WORLD
ETHNOGRAPHY

Editor

Aslan Gasimov

Authors
Aslan Gasimov
Ayan Karimova
Elshan Salayev
Lamiya Akhundova
Zarosh Allahverdiyeva
Lamiya Mustafayeva
Nigar Abdullazade
Nihad Mammadov
Aytaj Azemmedova
Senuber Allahverenova

Annotation

This book was made by students of BSU, Faculty of History, on the purpose of resolving source problems in English sections of high school on the studying of Ethnography. Classification of World nations by geographically and by language is held, also some notes about Azerbaijani ethnography is written in the book.

CONTENTS

INTRODUCTION

Ethnography is the systematic study of people, their ethnic identities, language, area where they settled, customs and traditions and more clearly their cultures. The term Ethnography derived, from Greek language - ethnos "folk, people, nation" and grapho "I write". In addition to the above-mentioned, Ethnography explores and research nations, establishment and development of ethnic communities, their distribution, cross-cultural, domestic relations, social structure, spiritual world and so on. West science learns Ethnography as Social Anthropolgy.

Each nation is unique, and has its own individual household. Ethnography study and learn processes and factors influence to the everyday life of the people and their household. Along with ethnographic study the culture of the people.

Culture itself is divided into two parts: the material and spiritual culture.The objects ,which created by human belong to the Material culture.To this group related: settlements, houses, temples, vehicles, tools, weapons, clothes, ornaments, dishes and etc.

The culture which based on human thoughts called Spiritual Culture: religion, customs, tradition, science, literature, art, music and so on. Included to this group. Each nation cultures have very different cultures and also the cultures arent at the same developmental level. Ethnography learning diversity and, also, similarities of the of the world cultures.

Humanity passed through a major development. During that time has undergone many changes in the history and culture. For example, people living in the structure of primitive clan and tribes united and created a unique culture.

Ethnography is carrying out scientific research in this area, too. It studies the people of the modern era and also the culture of the peoples of ancient times and also the nation, which has been dissapeared.

Ethnography as a science always related to nature and humanitarian sciences. Ethnography as an independent science began to formalize in the XIX century in Western Europe and America.

Ethnography's unique contribution to qualitative methods is that it deeply examines the context in which activities occur, usually involving work by the researcher with participants as they go about their daily lives. An ethnographer also describes a situation by asking multiple people about an event, or by analyzing multiple types of documentation, such as policies or historical records.

The father of History-Herodotus described in his nine books not only history but also the ethnos of the people, their culture, religion, customs and daily life. In his book of "History" we can find this kind of information with an amazing description about Persian nation. In the beginning of description of the Firstly he wants to show us daily life of Persian nation, because he tried to describe Persian war more accurately to the readers. As it turned out, Herodotus invented a new literary genre: history. He did so by integrating the results of empiricist ethnographic and topographic research into epic, and writing this in prose. This combination was revolutionary.[1]

Y. V. Bromley was one of the greatest representatives of the Ethnography. He brought a new term and new knowledge to this area, which called "Dualist theory of the ethnos». In 1973 Bromley in his work named "Ethnos and Ethnography"[2] and in his book, which was printed in 1981 "The Modern Problems of Ethnography: articles on theories and history"[3] wrote, that "Ethnography is about ethnic unions". Y. V. Bromley considered that humanity, developing according to the social general laws and splits into a large number of historical communities, among which a special place is occupied by ethnic group, as a special kind of human integration.

Starting with the ethnography of the Turkic-speaking peoples (Altay, Khakassia, Yakutsk) Tokarev subsequently became interested in the social organization and cultural history of the Australian Aborigines, Native American nations, the ethnography of the peoples of Europe, ethno genesis, material and spiritual culture of the peoples of the Caucasian and Russian region. The result of his many years of work was a series of monographs and one of the important book of Ethnography science – "The history of foreign ethnography (1978)"[4].

The object of the main learned the science of Ethnography is ethnos. As we noted in ethnos means nation.

---

[1] Heredot. "Tarix" // tərcümə P. Xəlilov. Bakı. 1998.

[2] *Бромлей Ю. В.* Этнос и этнография. — *Москва. 1973*

[3] Бр*омлей Ю. В.* Современные проблемы этнографии: очерки теории и истории. — Москва. 1981

[4] Токарев С.А. История зарубежной Этнографии. – Москва. 1978.

For the formation of an ethnic community each ethnic groups need certain indications. The basis for the formation of a nation- common language, common ethnic, territorial, domestic and commonality of culture and origin community.[5]

Language - We use Language to express our thoughts, emotions, to learn communicate with each-others and to share culture with each-others. Each person has individual ways of communication. All countries have their own national language, which formed through the hundreds and thousands of years. On the planet there are between 2,500 and 7,000 languages. Also some nations speak in the language of other nation and some nations speak two languages. At the same time there are International languages or World Languages. A world language is a language that is spoken internationally and is learned and spoken by a large number of people as a second language. A world language is characterized not only by the total number of speakers (native and second language speakers), but also by its geographical distribution, as well as use in international organizations and diplomatic relations.

Here are the main 5 International Languages (according to 2016's sources):

	Language	Number of speakers
1	Chinese	1.2 billion

[5] Həvilov H. A. Dünya xalqlarının Etnoqrafiyası. – Bakı 1998.

Common daily life and culture – Culture is the characteristics and knowledge of a particular group of people, defined by everything from language, religion, cuisine, social habits, music and arts. The word "culture" derives from a French term, which in turn derives from the Latin "colere," which means to tend to the earth and grow, or cultivation and nurture. "It shares its etymology with a number of other words related to actively fostering growth" Cristina De Rossi, an anthropologist at Barnet and Southgate College in London, told Live Science.

2	English	500 million
3	Spanish	425 million
4	Arabic	300 million
5	Russian	171 million

Ethnic area - The place where nation formed and settled. Sometimes the ethnic group of the people began their formation in one area but because of the historical, political changes and also nature disasters began movement of the people from one area to another. By the changing the Ethnic area sometime culture dies or began assimilation with different ethnic groups, which brought to a new ethnic group of the people on the new area. Many countries are largely populated by immigrants, and the culture is influenced by the many groups of people that now make up the country. This is also a part of growth. As the countries grow, so does its cultural diversity.

Ethnic identity - The extent to which one identifies with a particular ethnic group. Refers to one's sense of belonging to an ethnic group and the part of one's thinking, perceptions, feelings and behavior that is due to ethnic group membership. The ethnic group tends to be one in which the individual claims heritage.

Formation of Ethnography as a science

Ethnography science begins to spread in the American countries in the middle of the XIX century. Russian Geographical Society was found in Russia in 1845, after this it began formation of ethnography also in the territory of Caucasus. In 1851 was formed Russian Geographical Society Caucasian department. This formation was a push to prosper and spread ethnography on the territory of Caucasus including Azerbaijan.

Officially ethnography was accepted as a new science in the territory of Azerbaijan from the 19th century but formally it was found in Azerbaijan territory in the middle ages. In the beginning of 19th century Azerbaijan was unified with Russian Empire that was new stage in all sciences and cultural life on the territory of Azerbaijan. From the end of 19th century Azerbaijani scientist began to write interesting facts and articles about Ethnography science, this shows that interest to this area began to increase. Evidence of this was that a number of articles about Azerbaijan Ethnography were printed in the 1828-1832 in "Transcaucasian Gazette". "Caucasus" newspaper which was printed from 1846 till 1917 also played huge role in the spreading of Azerbaijan Ethnography on the territory of Caucasus. The authors, which studied the history of the territory of Azerbaijan were: V. N. Grigoriev, O. S. Evetskini, P. P. Zubov, the authors of "Review" (Obozreniye) V. S. Legkobytov, P.P.Zubarev, A.Q. Janowski. In 1833 was published "Statistical description of the province of Nakhichevan" by V.N.Grigoriev. One of the greatest books of this area at that time was published in 1835 by P.P.Zubov "The picture of the Caucasus region". In the 4th chapter of this book you can find ethnographic description of Shaki, Baku, Quba, Shirvan and Talish.[6]

In particular, in the middle of the nineteenth century as a result of realization of settling of stock-breeder tribes in villages the remains of community relations is protected more, so during the settling location on the kinship principles is observed strictly. As the process of settling was going among winter camps, the newly created villages were formed with exclusively relative patronymic groups. As a result, the formed customs and traditions had common features for all peoples.

Ethnography begins properly only with the twentieth century and two entirely independent intellectual developments, one British, the other North American. The first was the emergence of the classical tradition of social anthropology in Britain, with people like Malinowski, Boas, Radcliffe-Brown and Evans-Pritchard. That most were British or worked in Britain (with the obvious exception of Boas) can be explained because of the close association between social anthropology and British colonialism. And while social anthropology might no longer be the handmaiden of

---

[6] Həvilov H. A. Azərbaycan Etnoqrafiyası. – Bakı. 1991.

colonialism, its origins were tied to the needs of the British Empire to understand the cultures and groups it was seeking to rule once the period of colonial conquest was completed and assimilation in the 'British family of nations' was possible. This explains why it emerged at the beginning of the twentieth century rather than in the heyday of colonial conquest in the nineteenth century. These anthropologists pioneered an approach that involved close acquaintance with preindustrial groups and cultures by close immersion and observation.

The second development was the work of the Chicago School in sociology which used observational techniques to explore groups on the margins of urban industrial society in the United States in the 1920s and 1930s. With the occasional exception, the focus was on the dispossessed, the marginal and the strange, a focus Erving Goffman later came to characterize as an attempt to address 'the standpoint of the hip outsider rather than the dull insider'.[7]

While social anthropology called this approach 'ethnography', sociologists tended to call it participant observation or field research, but it meant much the same thing in the way research was conducted. There are some differences between these two intellectual pillars, but many similarities. The task of each was 'cultural description', and while social anthropology sought to explore pre-industrial groups and cultures, requiring ethnographers to adopt an initial research role as an outsider, the groups studied by the Chicagoans were only slightly less unfamiliar and strange to middle-class, Middle Western Americans, and their research role as an

---

[7] Brewer J. D. Ethnography. – Philadelphia. 2000.

'insider' was not guaranteed. Since then, of course, ethnography has moved into other social sciences, notably education, health studies and social work, and the differences between sociological and social anthropological uses of ethnography have widened, despite the fact that social anthropology now parallels sociology in a focus on urban and industrialized settings.

Sources and methods of Ethnography. The main sources of Ethnography consist of Research Observations. These sources are divided into 3 groups:

1. Direct observation.
2. Activity of ethnographer in the life of local population.
3. Interview with people, who gives information.

The information collected by mentioned methods are being included into field diaries of ethnographer. Also researcher takes different kind of photos, collects objects of material culture like dishes, clothes and so on.

There are two main methods of researching and getting new information and sources:

1. Expedition - It continues from 10 day till 3 months. Using this method ethnographer goes to the place where is in his interest. He observes household and culture of the people in the village. This method has short time, but ethnographer can collect lots of cultural material.
2. Stationer – By this method ethnographer stays and lives with the people of the village or city in his research, and learns material and spiritual culture,

household of the locals. Sometimes it can take 10-15 years of ethnographer.

CLASSIFICATIONS OF WORLD NATIONS

Different kinds of classifications are used for distinguishing of world nations from each-other and classifying them. Mainly, they are geographical, anthropological, economic-cultural type, religious and language classifications. Along with them, there are classification methods for the types of ethnic unions, socio-economical development levels of the nations, for the number of people and etc.[8]

Geographical classification: Each nation has own ethnic zone. The concept of an ethnic zone embraces the formation of nations in itself. Different nations formed in different geographical territories, migrated over time to time, changed their places and occupied new lands. As we know, Eastern Africa is a cradle of the human type. As a result of the historical development, the humans migrated from Africa to the other areas, with the emergence of Homo sapiens in Upper Paleolithic period, the humans could settle all areas which were suitable for the living. Together with the appropriation of new territories, the process of the shifting of human groups happened rapidly. Because of the increasing of population and the depletion of natural sources, clans and tribes left their lands, captured the lands of the other ones and assimilated them.

During that time they migrated not only in the land, but also through the sea. Gradually, the ethnicity of the countries began to change. During the history of mankind, some ethnic transferences were so fast, especially. Being more large and mass transferences, mainly, happened during Capitalism. Firstly, the invaders and colonizers, then the unemployed came from Western Europe to America, Southern Africa and Australia. So about last 3-4 centuries, the ethnicity of some areas of the world, especially, the nations of Australia and America changed more seriously. Eventually, we can come to the result that, the classification of the nations is not only an occupation of the human groups over political map, also the

---

[8] Quliyeva N. Etnoqrafiya və Etnologiya – Bakı. 2009.

factor which marks the occupation process of the area by the humans.

Usually, the nations who live within the borders of country for a while, regardless of their genesis, as a result of connections among one another, create similar household and culture forms. For example, Caucasian nations, have different languages and genesis, but living in neighboring territories, emerged lots of similar features of the cultural-household forms, for example; all-Caucasian wearing type, especially, the similarity of male wearing, weapon, tradition and folklore.

Historical ethnographic area is an area where historically, general cultural-household features of the nations are formed, such as Middle East, Latin America, Southern Europe, Caucasia and etc. While classifying the nations as geographical side, they are classified according to the historical-ethnographic areas. Historical-ethnographic area is a historical category. The nations who settle over a certain area, in contact, with one another but different for the direction and level of the socio-economical development, language and race, are related to historical-ethnographic area.[9]

"Great migration of the nations" led to the formation of modern ethnicity of Europe, Asia and Northern America. This process covers IV-IX centuries. Mainly, the process was related with the mass migrations and attacks of the Hun tribes from Asia to Europe. At the end of Middle Ages, the Great Discovery Age, discovery of New World-America, Australia and other areas, led to the migration of the nations to there and

---

[9] Həvilov H. A. Dünya xalqlarının Etnoqrafiyası. Bakı. 1998.

also the slaves who were came from Africa to work, participated in the formation of the nations.

Economic-cultural types: The world nations are classified for the differences of cultural-economic types as follows. The term cultural-economic (or economic-cultural) is complex features of the culture and economy of different nations who have the same or close development level, live in the similar natural-geographical condition. These types are related to the production methods of the society. In different historical periods, only production method marked the relation between the human and nature. In different socio-economical situations, the same cultural-economic types could appear among the nations who were not in contact with one another and lived so far. The differences among cultural-economic types show itself in agricultural activity of people, also in the material and spiritual elements of the culture. Social structure of different nations is defined with their own cultural-economic types. At the same time, these types reflect the level of productive forces of the society. These types are historical category. These cultural-economic types are divided into three groups for the level of productive forces. The first group includes hunting, gathering and partly fishing which have great economical importance, the second group - hoe planting and cattle-breeding; the third group - plough farming.

We can observe all three types of economic-cultural types in most of nation's life. These types play main role in the economic and household life of the nations, but sometimes they can be remains of the past.[10]

---

[10] Бромлей Ю. В., Марков Г. Е. Этнография. – Москва. 1982,

Religious classification: while mentioning about classification of the nations we have to look the religious divisions. In ancient periods, the humans related the natural events, illnesses and etc. with supernatural forces. So as a result of that, the religions emerged. Emergence of the religion was about the weakness of humans to natural forces. In fact, the humans could not understood real events, so they related all about different ghosts, gods and other creators.

Now over the world, there are international religions such as; Christianity, Islam, Buddhism and national religions such as Judaism, Hinduism, Shinto, Confucianism and hundreds of small ones.

Language classification

A language family is a grouping of linguistically linked languages, stemming from a common ancestral mother-language called Protolanguage. Most languages in the world belong to a specific family. Languages that have no demonstrable relation with others, and cannot be classified within a specific family, are generally known as language isolates.

There are two kinds of classification of languages practiced in linguistics: **genetic (or genealogical) and typological.** The purpose of genetic classification is to group languages into families according to their degree of diachronic relatedness. For example, within the Indo-European family, such subfamilies as Germanic or Celtic are recognized; these subfamilies comprise German, English, Dutch, Swedish, Norwegian, Danish, and others, on the one hand, and Irish, Welsh, Breton, and others, on the other. So far, most of the languages of the world have been grouped only tentatively into families, and many of the classificatory schemes that have been proposed will no doubt be radically revised as further progress is made.

A typological classification groups languages into types according to their structural characteristics. The most famous typological classification is probably that of isolating, agglutinating, and inflecting (or fusional) languages, which was frequently invoked in the 19th century in support of an evolutionary theory of language development. Roughly speaking, an isolating language is one in which all the words are morphologically unanalyzable (i.e., in which each word is composed of a single morph); Chinese and, even more strikingly, Vietnamese are highly isolating. An agglutinating language (e.g., Turkish) is one in which the word forms can be segmented into morphs, each of which represents a single grammatical category. An inflecting language is one in which there is no one-to-one correspondence between particular word segments and particular grammatical categories. For example, the Latin suffix -is represents the combination of categories "singular" and "genitive" in the word form hominis "of the man," but one part of the suffix cannot be assigned to "singular" and another to "genitive," and -is is only one of many suffixes that in different classes (or declensions) of words represent the combination of "singular" and "genitive."

Areal Classification of Language. A term used in dialectology for any geographical region isolated on the basis of its linguistic characteristics. The study of the linguistic properties of 'areas' – the analysis of the divergent forms they contain, and their historical antecedents – is known as areal linguistics. An areal classification would establish areal types (or groups), such as the Scandinavian languages, or the London-influenced dialects – cases where it is possible to show certain linguistic features in common as a result of the proximity of the speech communities. Such a classification often cuts across that made on purely historical grounds. It is often possible to identify a focal area – the region from which these linguistic characteristics have spread to the area as a whole (as in the case of London) – and several other significant parts of an area have been terminologically distinguished, e.g. the transitional areas which occur between adjacent areas, the relic areas which preserve linguistic features of an earlier stage of development. Areal linguistics is contrasted with non-areal differences in language use, e.g. contrasts between male and female speech, and between some social varieties. Areal linguistics is a way of classifying languages based on their regional location. It is not possible to fit every single language into a family structure, yet some languages do share common features which we can put down to things such as borrowing (due to close proximity or prolonged exposure). [11]

---

[11] http://studopedia.org/8-240370.html

NATIONS OF ASIA

Continent Eurasia is the biggest mainland in the world according to its area and the number of population. It is consisted of 2 continents: Europe and Asia. The Chinese have a proverb, "Tong chuang yi meng," which translates roughly as "Two people might share the same life, but they will still have different dreams." Applied to Asia and Europe, this can be understood as meaning that although Asians and Europeans live on the same planet, they undoubtedly have different ideas concerning their future prospects and their role in the world.

Some clarification of the designation of "Asia" or "Asian" is necessary in light of the vast amount of variations that exists across different cultures and societies within Asia. Asia represents the countries in the regions of East Asia (China, Japan, and Korea etc.), South Asia (India, Pakistan, Nepal, Bangladesh and Sri Lanka etc.), Southeast Asia (Vietnam, Laos, and Cambodia etc.), Central Asia, North Asia and West Asia.

There is an abundance of ethnic groups in Asia, with adaptations to the climate zones of the continent which include arctic, subarctic, temperate, subtropical or tropical, as well as extensive desert regions in Central and Western Asia. The ethnic groups have adapted to mountains, deserts, grasslands and forests, while on the coast of Asia resident ethnic groups have adopted various methods of harvest and transport. Some groups are primarily hunter-gatherers, some practice transhumance (nomadic lifestyle), others have been agrarian for millennia and others becoming industrial or urban. Some groups or countries in Asia are completely urban (e.g. Hong Kong and Singapore). The largest countries in Asia with regard to population are the People's Republic of China, India, Pakistan, Japan and South Korea. Colonization of Asian ethnic groups and states by European peoples beginning in the XVI century, reaching its peak in the late XIX and early XX centuries (except in the former Soviet Union which, which was dissolved in 1990).

Colonial occupations influenced negatively to social-economy, but positively to the cultural development. We can meet all races in Asia. But mongoloid and europoid races are in majority in this continent. There are also representatives of papuas, Melanesian, pygmy-negritos and austroloid races. Peoples who live in Asia speak in China-Tibet, Indian-Europe,

Semit-Hamit, Altay, Austronesian language families. Population is more than 3 billion.

The language families of Asia Most language families have several branches. But it is a universal feature of human languages that they change through time. This process happens in different ways, at different places and in different social groups. However, it may be misleading to say that *languages change*, because what happens is rather that *human beings change their languages*.

They change in many ways. The meanings of words are changed, the pronunciations of words are changed, new words are adopted, old words are discarded, inflections come and disappear in the structure of phrases and sentences are changed and etc.

Linguists don't agree about the numbers of language families in the world. Some linguists may be on the opinion that some two language groups are related that they are branches of a single family, while others reject the evidence meant to prove the relatedness, concluding that the groups constitute separate language families. In this part of the chapter we will give short descriptions of some of the most important language families in Asia. There is no general agreement about the number of families or their internal structures. We will, however, try to express traditional mainstream views.

Sino-Tibetan: Its history is associated with Neolithic and Bronze Age developments in China itself, and today it is one of the major world language families in terms of population numbers. The Sino-Tibetan languages are spoken throughout China and Myanmar/Burma and in parts of India, Thailand, Laos, and Vietnam. The archeological and linguistic evidence suggests that the ancestors of the Sino-Tibetan speaking people lived in the central plains of the valley of the Huanghe (Yellow River).

Sino-Tibetan includes both the **Sinitic** and **Tibeto-Burman** languages. Today more than one billion people speak in Sinitic (the Chinese dialects) as their mother-tongue. According to most scholars of China, here include not only these two branches, but also Tai and Hmong-Mien as well. They consider that **Sinitic (Chinese)** branch consists of different dialects which can be considered as one single language. The linguists believe that the Chinese actually is not a one language, it is a language family. 14 main languages include here. The most famous ones are: Mandarin, Wu, Canton, Min etc.

The Chinese distinguish the written language and speaking language from each other. They called the regional dialects as *fangyen*. The differences between these dialects let us to say that they are actually different languages. Despite all of these differences their writing system is common. This writing system which appeared in the 3rd century BC was configured based on Mandarin language in XX century.

Tibeto-Burman branch of the language family spread over a large area from Tibetan plateau in the north to Malay peninsula in the south and from northern Pakistan in the west to northeastern Vietnam in the east. While languages of Chinese (Sinitic) branch have a large numbers of speakers, the languages of Tibeto-Burman branch have a small number of speakers. There are approximately 389 different languages within the Tibeto-Burman branch. The languages of Tibeto-Burman branch are spoken in Burma (Myanmar), Thailand, Laos, Southern China, Tibet, Bhutan, Nepal and Eastern India.

Indo-European language family: As we know, there are two branch of Indo-European language family. But here we will mention about Asian branch of it. In the Asian branch of Indo-European language family, there include Indian, Persian and Armenian languages. In 1813 Thomas Young called the language family as "Indo-European" because of it has spread from Western Europe to India. Today it is mother-tongue for more than 2.5 billion people.

Indo-Aryan or Indic is a subgroup of Indo-Iranian branch of Indo-European language family. Today it has about one billion speakers and spread mostly in the territories of Northern and Middle India, Pakistan, Afghanistan, Bangladesh, Nepal, Sri-Lanka and Maldives. The most important ones among Indo-Aryan languages are Indian, Hindustani, Bengali, Punjabi, Gujarati and Sanskrit.

Ural-Altaic: Ural-Altaic or by the other name Turanian is a language family which it is spoken in America and Eurasia. The number of the speakers of this language family reach to 750 million today. Ural-Altay language family divide into two branches: Uralic and Altaic. Altaic branch spreaded in Eastern, Northern, Central and Western Asia and also Eastern Europe. The languages of more than 700 million people belong to Altaic branch and they are spoken from the south of Ural Mountains to the Japan Sea. Turkic, Mongolic, Tungusic languages are considered the subdivisions of this branch. Also the Japanese and Korean is included to this branch but it is a disputable issue for linguistics. But recently the comparative researches show that Japanese and Korean also includes to this branch.

Major religions in Asia

Asia has been the birthplace of many famous major religions in the world. As we know, Asia is the largest and most populous continent of the world. Because of its wide area, it is the home of large variety of religions.

Hinduism. "Hindu" is a word that comes from the name of the Indus River, which also gives the name of the modern state of India. Most Hindu people of the world have roots in the region. The world is home to over 900 million Hindus. Most of them live in India, a country with 1.166 billion people, of whom about 80 percent are Hindu. Large numbers of people who follow the Hindu religion are also found in Nepal, Bangladesh, Indonesia, Sri Lanka, Malaysia, and beyond.

Hinduism is the third-largest religion in the world, after Christianity and Islam. As you read through this chapter, think about the many ways in which Hinduism compares and contrasts with other faiths you have learned about. Hinduism is a tradition that means many things and has many variations. It is not a single, unified, centralized religion the way Roman Catholicism is. It is very individualized and has no formal church and no single authority. It has no founder and no fixed doctrines.

The Indus River flows from the Himalayas to the Arabian Sea through what is now Pakistan. Most Hindus live on the Indian subcontinent, but others are part of the Indian diaspora. "Diaspora" means "scattering of seeds." The Indian diaspora dates back to Britain's control within the region from 1858 until 1947.

Ritual Bathing in the Ganges. Every 12 years, a sacred ritual takes place at Prayag, near Allahabad, on the Ganges in northern India. At each festival, millions of people bathe in the sacred Ganges River to come closer to the source of life, to wash away their sins, and to cleanse both their bodies and their spirits. For Hindus, however, a pilgrimage to the Ganges is not considered necessary, but highly desirable.

History of Hinduism. Hinduism is one of the oldest religions in the world. For centuries, the native religion of ancient India was known as ***sanatan dharma, "the way of life."*** It was not until centuries later that the name "Hinduism" was first used. Hinduism can be described as evolving over three historical periods. During each period, Hinduism adapted to new situations, but kept traces of the previous periods.

Pre-Vedic period. An ancient civilization thrived in the fertile valley of the Indus River in the third and second millennium before the birth of Christ—about 2500 to 1500 BC.

Historians and archaeologists still have many questions about the Indus Valley Civilization. One reason is that the Indus Valley Civilization's language has not been deciphered. However, scholars do know that :

• most of the people lived in cities—cities that were impressively complex, built with bricks, and that included sophisticated drainage and sewage systems

• it was a matriarchal society—one in which women, especially mothers, took a leading role

• people worshipped a mother goddess—whom some later Hindu deities resemble.

Scholars believe that later Hindu deities evolved from goddess images of this period.

Vedic period. The Vedic period, which began around 1500 BC until 600 BC, is named for the fi rst sacred writings of Hinduism, the Vedas, because scholars think those writings were collected during this period.The language of the Vedas is Sanskrit, and **"Veda"** is the Sanskrit word for knowledge. Rituals during the period focused on prayers, the elements of nature, and animal sacrifices.

The Uphanishadic period. The third and fi nal period in the history of Hinduism began around 600 BC. From about 600 to 200 BC:

• ancient India's culture was unified

• Hinduism both accepted the Vedas and added to them, with the Upanishads

• worship began in temples

The Upanishads are interpretations of the Vedas added to the end of each. With these powerful additions, Hinduism as we know it emerged. The Upanishads moved Hinduism from a focus on sacrificial practices to a philosophical and meditative way of life—a focus more on the inner self.

Rituals. Puja is the most common form of Hindu worship. It involves worshipping one or more Hindu deities. The image of a deity is called a **murti**. It is believed to contain the particular aspect of the essence of the Supreme Being or of the one God. Hindus believe that there is only one God or Supreme Being, but that this Being has many different forms. The main place for offering puja is in the home. Whether at home or in a temple, the ritual involves sounds, light, washing, food, scent, and prayers.

Most Hindu families have a place of worship in their homes—a room, a corner, or an alcove set aside as a shrine. To start, worshippers remove their shoes, a bell is rung to summon the presence of the murti, a lamp is lit, and incense is burned. The murti is washed and decorated with garlands or flower petals. A special powder is mixed with water to make a red paste. A small amount of this paste is placed on the foreheads of the murti and the worshippers. The worshippers make an offering of fruit, light, flowers or sweets to the murti. The lamp is moved around the murti in a clockwise direction to indicate the presence of God. The devotees then each place both hands above the lamp flame and touch their foreheads, showing that they are receiving the deity's blessing. Any food that has been part of the puja must be eaten by everyone present, to honor the deity and share in the deity's power. At the end of the ritual, some Hindus turn around three times to show that they remember God is all around them.

Hindus visit the ***mandir*** to offer prayers and devotion any time or day of the week, just as they might drop in on friends for a visit. A Hindu temple is a complex of shrines, each devoted to a different deity. The main deity is enshrined in the centre. Temples can be very large, and able to accommodate hundreds of thousands of devotees. As worshippers enter the temple, they remove their shoes and wash their hands. Then they approach the shrine to make an offering. As they approach, they ring a bell to announce their arrival to the murti.

The Caste system In traditional Hindu society:

• each person had a certain social position in life

• all life was arranged as a hierarchy, from highest to lowest

• performing good deeds and following their assigned code of behavior determined whether people had earned the right to be born at a higher level

These traditional beliefs were expressed in Hindu society's division into castes. Roles, jobs, social standing, and religious structures were organized according to the hierarchy of castes. The caste system is said to have come to ancient India around 1500 BC, with the Aryans. The caste system had four groups: priests, defenders of the realm, business people, and farmers. More recently, another caste developed the **Untouchables** or outcastes.

1. Brahmans: This is the priestly caste. Their role is to study and teach in matters of faith, especially the Vedas. They lead most key rituals.

2. Kshatriyas*:* This has been called the warrior caste. Their role is to protect the people and run a fair government.

3. Vaishyas*:* This caste consists of producers—traders, merchants, farmers, artists, and businesspeople. This group has traditionally taken care of the economic needs of the community.

4. Sudras*:* This is the lowest caste. Their main purpose is to serve the three higher castes. This group includes unskilled workers, servants, and anyone doing menial work.

5. Untouchables*:* Also called ***"outcastes"*** people in this group are considered outsiders: they may not interact in any way with members of the four castes. Traditionally, they do the dirtiest work in society and live apart, in small communities. However, this situation is changing. There are now quotas in place to ensure that members of this caste have access to better jobs.

Buddism. The bases of the Buddism come from the ideas of Siddharta Gautama in 6th century BC. Siddharta Gautama lived in the present-day border area between India and Nepal in the 6th century before Christ. His exact birth date is unknown. Because the life of the historical Buddha is inseparable from the legend.

Buddhists believe the *"Nirvana"*, which means enlightenment. Actually, "Buddism" or "Buddhist" is a term used in the West. But in East the term of *"Nangpa"*(in Tibetan language)is used. Today about 500 million Buddhists live in the world. Buddism has three main branches: **Theravada**, **Mahayana** and **Vajrayana**. Theravada is the oldest one applied in mostly Thailand, some parts of India and south eastern Asia. Mahayana branch is applied in China, Taiwan, Vietnam, Korea, Japan. Finally, Vajrayana branch of Buddism is applied in Tibet, most parts of India, some parts of China and Japan, Asian Turkic Republics.

Islam. The Muslim world of Asia has been experienced the Islamic revival. There are about 1.2 billion Muslims in the world, of which 60% live in Asia. But only 15% of them are Arabs, while approximately one third live in South Asia. The four nations with the largest Muslim populations, Indonesia (194 million), India (150 million), Pakistan (145 million), and Bangladesh (130 million), are in Asia. China also has a population of 39 million Muslims. Despite this, the Muslims of Asia are perceived to be on the periphery of the Islamic core based in the Arab Middle East. Muslims are a majority in Kirgizstan, Uzbekistan, Tajikistan and Turkmenistan in Central Asia, Afghanistan, Pakistan, and Bangladesh in South Asia and

Malaysia, Brunei, and Indonesia in Southeast Asia. There are also significant minority populations in India, Thailand, and the Philippines. Sizable Muslim communities are also found in Sri Lanka, China, Burma, and Singapore.

The majority of Muslims are Sunnis, while 10-15% are Shiite. This difference stems from disagreement over the succession to the prophet Mohammad. In South and Southeast Asia, Shiites are a significant portion of the population in only Afghanistan and Pakistan.

The relatively few Muslims of Northeast Asia are found in China for the most part. China is home to an estimated 17.5 to 36 million Muslims. The largest, most concentrated group is the Uyghurs of Xinjiang Province in western China. The Uighur minority has experienced unrest of an Islamic character in recent years.

Different cultures, traditions and lifestyles in Asia

More than 3/4 of the Southeast Asia population is agriculture-based. Twice as much fish is consumed in this region compared to other forms of animal protein, reflecting the long coastlines and river environments of Southeast Asia. The staple food throughout the region is rice, which has been cultivated for thousands of years. Rice serves as the basic staple food for more than half of the world's population today.

Daily meals and elaborate feasts characterize all Southeast Asian culinary cultures. Cooking is economically efficient as people use wok cooking, which requires a low amount of fuel and makes deep-frying easy. Also, meat and vegetables are typically chopped into small pieces prior to cooking, which mean that food cooks very quickly. Most food is cooked by quick blanching or stir-frying and steaming. Southeast Asians are concerned with nutrition, economy, and ease of preparation as it relates to their food.

In Asia, there are different styles of eating food. In India and the Middle East, as well as Southeast Asia, people eat food with their hands. It is a very direct way to experience the texture of the food, and people normally wash their hands before and after each meal. Normally, only the right hand is used, so that one knows to keep it especially clean. Generally, the foods to be eaten are placed on plates in the center of the mat or table, and people take food in small portions as they eat.

Indian cooking has influenced much of Southeast Asia. However, Indian cooking varies throughout the country and according to ethnic and religious preference. Most know that Muslims do not eat pork, and that the month of Ramadan (the ninth month of the Muslim lunar calendar) is a time of fasting for Muslims all over the world. Muslims may neither eat nor drink during the daylight hours of this month.

Social and economic activities associated with feasting include rice harvesting, an important community event that is celebrated in dance and ritual. Symbols of rice are found in textiles, such as batik in Indonesia. Women generally prepare rice for each meal. The development of wet-rice, or irrigated rice cultivation systems in Southeast Asia, led to the continual development of large-scale civilizations, societies, and hierarchies of nobles, commoners, and dependents. Similarly, the Spice Trade, focused in eastern Indonesia, eventually led to the European colonization and intervention into Southeast Asia. Spices were in great demand in India and China, as well as Europe.

Rice is the basis of Southeast Asian food, and in many languages a common greeting is "Have you eaten yet?" The verb for "to eat" is often the same as the verb "to eat rice". Rice is used for fuel oil, rice-paper, alcoholic drinks, tea, all manner of foods, cosmetics, medicines, and magical potions. Typically, a small portion of food is offered to the gods, ancestral spirits, and other beings during ritual sacrifices at major ceremonies or even before common, everyday meals. Food can even have an importance in peace relations between neighboring countries, such as is the case in Thailand and Malaysia. The Muslim Malays raise pigs for the Thai Buddhists, who in turn raise cattle for Malays. Although differentiation in culture and religion exist throughout this region, the cooperative food trading system has helped attain peace and forge alliances between neighboring peoples.

Status of women. Economic, social, and political developments in Asia have brought with them profound changes in the status of women. In general, women's conditions have improved with economic development and social and political change that favors equality and individual rights. At the same time, cultural traditions, especially those related to family life, continue to have a strong influence on the status of women in the region.

Until recently in most Asian countries, few women attended secondary school or university, and few worked outside the home. Over the past 50 years, larger and larger proportions of women have completed primary and secondary school. The proportion of women attending university, although much smaller, is also growing. More recently, women have started taking up paid employment in greater numbers, particularly in the manufacturing, clerical, and service sectors.

Over the past 50 years, women's life expectancy has improved across the region, overtaking men's life expectancy in nearly all countries. Yet during early childhood, girls are still more likely to die than boys in some Asian countries.

Demographic dynamics of Asia

"Demography is destiny" stated the XIX century French sociologist Auguste Comte. If that is so, Asia must certainly hold the key to the world's economic future. In terms of the size of its population and growth, no other region looms as large. As a region, Asia is home to the world's largest numbers of consumers and producers. It enjoys, and will continue to enjoy, a favorable ratio of workers to retirees and dependent children. Yet no single adjective can describe any one Asian country, as it is a collection of some of the most diverse nations on earth.

Asia has been the world's largest region in terms of population throughout history and is virtually certain to remain so far into the future. Asia is home to 4 billion people.

The key to Asia's present and future demographic development lies in the Total Fertility Rate, or TFR. The TFR is the average number of children a woman would have in her lifetime if the country's overall birth rate were to remain constant. For example, there are about 27 million births per year in India, which equals a birth rate of 24 births per 1,000 inhabitants. At that rate, women in India would average about three births each in their lifetime, or a TFR of three. The TFR has the advantage of expressing fertility in terms of the number of children, or "family size."

All across Asia, the number of people age 65 and above is expected to grow dramatically over the next 50 years. For the region as a whole, the population in this age group will increase by 314 percent—from 207 million in 2000 to 857 million in 2050.

In 2000, the average age in Asia was 29 years. An estimated 6 percent of the region's total population were age 65 and older, 30 percent were under age 15, and 64 percent were in the working-age group of 15 to 64 years.

Japan has the oldest population in Asia, with 17 percent age 65 and older, and the most rapidly aging population in the world. The United Nations medium scenario anticipates that 29 percent of Japanese will be 65 or older by 2025 and 36 percent will be 65 or older by 2050. Bangladesh, by contrast, has the youngest population of any major country in the region, with 3 percent 65 or older in 2000. But even Bangladesh and Asia's other young populations will experience rapid population aging during the coming decades. Bangladesh's 65 and older population is projected to rise to 5 percent in 2025 and 11 percent in 2050.

In most countries of Asia, as in the rest of the world, older women outnumber older men, particularly in the oldest age groups. Today, among the population age 55 and above, there are about 90 men in Asia for every 100 women. Among those ages 75 and above, there are only about 70 men for every 100 women. This is a persistent feature of Asia's population that is not expected to change much over the next 50 years.

Greater employment opportunities. For many Asians, early retirement is a welcome component of general improvements in the standard of living. Today, mandatory retirement ages range from a high of 65 in Japan to a low of 55 in India, Indonesia, and Singapore. China, Vietnam, Pakistan, and Sri Lanka impose a lower retirement age for women than for men, despite the fact that women generally live longer than men and may spend many years in old age without employment.

NATIONS OF EUROPE

The acception of Europe as a part of the Earth is dealt the important role of peoples who settled in Europe. Etymology of the name of Europe has only geographical mean, it was Greek word "Europe" which means "western country". It is the western part of Eurasia. In the territory spread nations who belong to the europoid race. According their characteristics europoid race divided into northern europoid and Sothern europoid subraces. Northern europoid race belong to Scandinavian countries' population. The population who belong to the southern europoid race spread in the southern Europe. In Europe four big group spread which belong to Indo-European language family: Romance, Slavic, Germanic, Celt language groups. Besides these branches there are small language groups like Basque and Albanian. In Europe live people who belong to Ural, Altaic and Semit-Hamit language families.

Slavs or Slavic language group. The biggest and the most settled nations in Europe are Slavs. The term ''Slavs'' designates an ethnic group of people who share a long-term cultural continuity and who speak a set of related languages known as the Slavic languages (all of which belong to the Indo-European language family). Little is known about Slavs before they are mentioned in Byzantine records of the VI century CE and most of what we know about them prior to this time is mainly derived from archaeological and linguistic studies. The Byzantine authors refer to the Slavs as ''Sclaveni''. Slavs divided into 3 groups:

1. Southern Slavs

2. Western Slavs
3. Eastern Slavs

South Slavs include the Bosniaks, Bulgarians, Croats, Macedonians, Montenegrins, Serbs and Slovenes. They are the main population of the Southeast European and Eastern European countries of Bulgaria, Bosnia and Herzegovina, Croatia, FYR Macedonia, Montenegro, Serbia and Slovenia. These nations mostly settled in Balkan Peninsula. Southern Slavs have ancient growing and cattle-breeding traditions. Southern Slavs have some different ancient holidays. Some of them are "obrok" and "the days of worm". These days are dedicated to worms and celebrated the first weeks of November. Besides these holidays we can observe the holiday which important in Bolgars and other Slavs was "the days of Trifon Zarezan". This holiday is celebrated on the 14th of February. Other holidays are "girls holiday", "the day of Georgiev".

The religious and cultural diversity of the region the South Slavs inhabit has had a considerable influence on their religion. Originally a polytheistic pagan people, the South Slavs have also preserved many of their ancient rituals and traditional folklore, often intermixing and combining it with the religion they later converted to. Today the majority of the South Slavs are Orthodox Christians-the most Bulgarians, Macedonians, Serbs and Croats are Roman Catholics. Bosniaks, other minor ethnic groups and sub-groups are Muslims. Some South Slavs are atheist, agnostic and non-religious.

South Slavs standard languages are Bosnian, Bulgarian, Croatian, Macedonian, Montenegrin, Serbian and Slovene. In addition, there are also other south Slavic languages which do not constitute official status in any republic.

West Slavic languages also divided into three sub-groups: Czecho-Slovak, Lechitic and Sorbian. West Slavic speaking nations are the Czechs, Slovaks, Poles, Kashubians, Silesians and Sorbs. They inhabit a contiguous area in Central Europe stretching from the north of the Baltic sea to the Sudetes and the Carpathian Mountains in the south, historically also across the Eastern Alps into Appennine peninsula and the Balkan peninsula.

The spiritual culture of western Slavs is rich traditional ceremonies. So in Poles and Slovaks "dojinka" and "objomka" are celebrated as national holiday. This is an ancient Slavic growing holiday and this holiday is celebrated in the months of August and September. The main aim of the celebration of this holiday is to increase the harvest. We can observe some holidays which belong to this period "the holiday of spring", "the holiday of youth", "tree of May" and etc. The most part of Poles, Czechs and Slovaks are Catholic.

East Slavic countries include the Russians, Belarusians and Ukrainians. Eastern Slavs are close one-another because of cultural characteristics. Common number of East Slavs approximately is 200 million. Nowadays more than 145 Russians, 46 million Ukrainians and over 10 million Belarusians live in East Slavic countries. In eastern Slavs have developed agriculture, cattle-breeding, especially keeping big-horned cattle. We can find ethnographic characteristics in their cloths. Eastern Slavs grow flax and get wool, labor. The main clothing type is shirt. Men wear shirts until their knees and women wear longer shirts. The shawls of Eastern Slavic countries are more interesting. Some differences have between shawls which the girls and the married women wear. Russians, Belarusians and Ukrainians are made garland from shawls. Eastern Slavs served in Pravaslaw church. The holidays which called "Ivan Kupola", "Maslenitsa", "Traitsa" are celebrated among eastern Slavs.

Germanic language group: The nations which belong to this group settled in Western, Central and Northern Europe including Northern Atlantic islands. Germans are Germanic ethnic group native to Central Europe, who share a common ancestry culture and history. The Germans emerged as an ethnicity during the Medieval Ages. The German ethnicity is linked to Germanic tribes of antiquity of Central Europe. The early Germans originated on the Northern German plain as well as Southern Scandinavia. By the 2nd century BC the number of Germans was significantly increasing and they began expanding into Eastern Europe and southward into Celtic territory.

According some characteristics features of language and culture these nations divided into two large groups: Northern Germanic nations (Scandinavians) and Western Germanic nations. Scandinavian nations include Swedish, Norwich, Danish and Farers. Agriculture developed in the area of forests and this is dealt with natural-geographical conditions. Swedish people have their own clothes and they wear these clothes only in wedding. The national clothes of Norwich are called "bunad". Woolen clothes are widely spread in Denmark. Traditional culture of Farers Island is close to Norwich culture

Western Germanic nations are Germans, Austrians, English, Dutch, Yiddish and others. Among these nations the most spread language is German and English language. All German nations called themselves as "Deutsch". This name came from the name of "Tevton" tribe which lived in the northern part of the country. In ancient times the tribes who lived in the southern part of the country called Aleman and with this tribe's name most of Roman nations called Germans as Aleman and English called them Germans. The traditional employment of Germans is cattle-breeding and growing. The national holidays and national cuisine of English are more interesting. The national meals of English which called "roast beef" and "beefsteak" are popular in most countries. Traditional spring holiday especially is celebrated in England only one day. In Germans holidays also are celebrated with great festivals.

According to the latest nationwide census Roman Catholics constituted 29.5% the total population of Germany followed by Evangelical Protestants at 27.9%. Other Christian denominations, other religions, atheists and not specified constituted 42.6% of the population nowadays.

Romance Nations. Romance peoples refer to societies influenced by Roman culture and speak Romance languages. Italian, Spanish, Corsican, French, Portuguese, Romanian and Moldovan are branches of Romance language group. Catalan also has taken on a political and cultural significance among the Romanian. By the name Romance indeed suggests the ultimate connection of these languages with Rome, the English word is derived from an old French form of Latin Romanicus used in the Medieval Ages to designate a vernacular type of Latin speech as well as literature written in the vernacular. By the beginning of the XXI century some 920 million people claimed a Romance language as their mother tongue, 300 million people as a second language.

The original Indo-European tribes of the Italic people settled in Neolithic times in the Italian peninsula. These tribes were historically divided between Latino-Faliscans, Osco-Umbrians, Veneti and Ligures. Italians are nations and ethnic group native to Italy who share a common Italian culture, ancestry and speak the Italian language as a mother tongue. In 2014 in addition to about 55 million Italians in Italy, Italian–speaking autonomous groups exist in neighboring countries: about half a million in Switzerland a large population in France and smaller groups in Slovenia and Croatia. Because of wide ranging diaspora about 5 million Italian citizens and nearly 80 million people of full or part Italian ancestry live outside of Italy, most notably in South America, North America, Australia and parts of Europe. Italians have greatly influenced and contributed to science, arts, technology, cuisine, sports jurisprudence and banking both abroad and worldwide. Italian people are generally known for their localism both regionalist and municipality attention to clothing and family values.

The French are ethnic group and nation who identified with the country of France. The modern French population is largely native-born and represents a fusion of many peoples of Celtic, Germanic, Latin and Slavic origins. Contrary to what has happened in many other countries, the immigrants have blended so well into existing French society that today is difficult to determine the ethnic origins of most French citizens. More ethnically prominent are the 20th century immigrants including an estimated 4 million foreigners mainly Portuguese, Spanish and Italians and many French citizens a large number of them Arabs who entered France in the 1960s from former French colonies in Algeria and sub-Saharan Africa. The French language is understood and spoken by the entire population, although other languages and dialects persist alongside French in peripheral areas. About 80% of the population belongs to the Roman Catholic Church. Protestants constitute less than 2% of the population, Jews about 1%, Muslims who have entered France recently from former North African colonies about 4%.

The Occitan people are ethnic group native to Occitania in Southern France. The Occitan language is still used to varying levels between 100,000 and 800,000 speakers in Southern France and Northern Italy. Since 2006 the Occitan language is recognized as one of the official languages in Catalonia, an autonomous region of Spain. The Occitans are concentrated in Occitania and also in big urban centers like Lyon, Paris, Turin and Barcelona.

Portuguese people are nations and ethnic group native to the country of Portuguese. According to the 2001 census there are about ten million people living in Portugal. Almost two-thirds of them live in the coastal fourth of the country, with the capital city Lisbon and its surrounding metropolitan area having the largest population with around two million people. Most of the current Portuguese population grew from the mixture of all the peoples who have inhabited and traded in the region over the centuries. The first to settle were the Iberians and over the years Celts, Romans, Germanic tribes, Jews and others migrated into the area and combined to develop people with unique physical characteristics. Most Portuguese have typical Mediterranean features like brown eyes, dark hair and height of less than 6 feet. Evidence of the Germanic can still be seen in the north of the country where taller, light-haired and light-eyed people are occasionally encountered. About 97% of the Portuguese population identified themselves as Roman Catholic, but other religions enjoy freedom of worship. Protestants constitute 1% of the populace and various other groups make up the remaining 2%. Although church and state are separated in the Constitution, the country's holidays, its moral and legal codes, health and educational systems are intervened with its Catholic heritage. The Portuguese are a deeply superstitious people whose formal Catholicism is profoundly intertwined with pre-Christian beliefs. Older rural women are expected to dress in black after the death of their husbands for about seven years. Western style clothing is the norm and people in the cities dress well. However vestiges of traditional garb such as berets for men and black shawls for women may still be seen in some rural areas.

Romanians are nations and ethnic group native to Romania that share a common Romanian culture, ancestry and speak the Romanian language as a mother language. The Romanian citizenship law legislated in March 1991 establishes the rights of the second and third generation descendants of Romanian citizens to obtain a Romanian citizenship, if they speak fluent Romanian and are able to demonstrate sufficient knowledge in Romanian history and culture. The origins of the Romanian language a Romance language can be traced back to the Roman colonization of the region. Almost 90% of all Romanians consider themselves religious. The vast majority are Eastern Orthodox Christians.

The Spanish are made up many nationalities or ethnicities: the Asturians, Galicians, Basques, Navarese, Valincians, Catalons, Andalusians, Aragonose and others. Today Spain's language with the exception of Basque, stem from the Vulgar Latin that was spoken in Hispania and which evolved into the modern Romance languages of the Iberian peninsula, including Castilian. Romance languages spoken in Spain include the official language Spanish or Castilian and the co-official regional languages Catalon in Catalonia and Galician in Galicia.

And also the spiritual life of the Romance speaking nations is rich different traditional holidays. "Christmas" and "New Year" is celebrated widely. For example, Italians in "New Year" throw the plates which not used in their homes and also they throw the ancient furniture. The biggest spring holiday is "Carnival". "Carnival" walking is held usually in February and March. "Easter" is the second largest spring holiday. In Spain the most beloved holiday is "Christmas". On the 1st of November is considered as a holiday for all holistic persons in Spain. In Spain is also held "Corrida" (a bullfight).

Celtic Nations. This group include the Irish (northern and southern Irish), Welsh (Wales), Scottish (in Scotland) and Bretons (in France). Celts were the ancient nations of Europe. The ancient Celts were various population groups living in several parts of Europe north of the Mediterranean region from the Late Bronze Age onwards. Given the name Celt by ancient writers these tribes often migrated and so eventually occupied territories from Portugal to Turkey. Most scholars agree that the Celtic culture first appeared in the Late Bronze Age in the area of the Upper Danube sometime around the 13th century BCE. These early Celts were known as the "Urnfield people" and they spoke a proto–Celtic language. By the 8th century BCE iron had replaced bronze working and the cultural group is then referred to by scholars as the "Hallstatt culture". The Hallstatt culture declined by the 5th century BCE, perhaps due to internal political tensions and economic difficulties. The next phase of Celtic development was carried out by a group known as the "La Tene culture". The prosperity of the La Tene in ancient France, Spain and wider Central Europe meant that they were able to challenge the contemporary Mediterranean cultures and so they appear for the first time in Classical history. From then on these peoples were widely referred to as Celts. The religion of the Celts led by a priesthood known as the Druids is described by ancient writers with some disdain as crude and violent.

The Celtic language is a branch of the Indo-European language family. Scholars have divided Celtic languages into two groups: Insular Celtic and Continental Celtic. The latter group was no larger widely spoken after the Roman imperial period and the only surviving examples of it are mentions in the works of Greek and Roman writers and some epigraphic remains such as pottery.

Baltic nations: The Baltic countries (also known as Baltic States) is north-eastern region of Europe containing the countries of Latvia, Lithuania and Estonia on the eastern shores of Baltic Sea. Baltic countries have its name for being bounded on the west and north by the Baltic Sea. Baltic countries usually are referred to the territories east of Baltic Sea which gained independence from the Russian Empire in the wake of World War I. The republics of Estonia, Latvia and Lithuania which became constituent republics of the former Soviet Union in 1940, regained their independence in 1991.

Latvia is a democratic, parliamentary republic located in Baltic region neighboring with Russia with population of 2.1 million. Latvia became independent in 1918 and was occupied by Soviet Union and Nazi Germany during the II World War and again by the Soviet Union after the Second World War until it regained its independence in 1991. Today Latvia is a member of both the European Union and North Atlantic Treaty Organization (NATO). Latvia is ranked as world's second greenest country and the Latvian capital Riga is the biggest city in the Baltic countries.

Lithuania is a parliamentary democracy on the eastern coast of the Baltic Sea and it is largest in Baltic countries. Lithuania has population about 3,2 million people it is the southern most of the 3 Baltic countries. The capital o Lithuania is Vilnius. Lithuania was the first Soviet republic to declare independence from the USSR. Today Lithuania is a member of NATO, the Council of Europe and the European Union.

Uralic Language family is spread in the North Eurasia. The most native speakers of Uralic languages are Finnish, Hungarian and Estonian people who had settled in Europe and created states. Finland is one of the best developed countries in the world. It has population about 5.5 million, staying roughly on the same level over the past two decades. Finland gained independence from Russian Empire in 1918. Finland is a parliamentary republic with a central government based in the capital Helsinki, local governments in 317 municipalities, and an autonomous region, the Aland Islands. Over 1.4 million people live in the Greater Helsinki metropolitan area, which produces a third of the country's GDP.

Hungary is situated in the East Europe. It was one of main states of Austria-Hungary Empire along with Austria. After WWI Hungary lost some parts of country`s territory. Nowadays it covers an area of 93,030 square kilometers, with about 10 million inhabitants. The official language is Hungarian, which is the most widely spoken Uralic language in the world. Hungary's capital is Budapest, a significant economic hub, classified as an Alpha- global city. Major urbanareas include Debrecen, Szeged, Miskolc and Pécs.

Estonia is a democratic parliamentary republic divided into 15 countries which has over 1,500 islands. Estonian capital and largest city is Tallinn. With a population of 1.29 million, it is one of the least-populous members of the European Union, Eurozone and the North Atlantic Treaty Organization. Geographically Estonia is on the north eastern edge of the European Union, bordering Russia and Latvia. Almost half of Estonia territory is covered by forests.

Nowadays, in Europe settled also Semitic-Hamitic people like Maltese, Jews and Arabian migrants. Arabs are generally migrated from North African states, which decades ago were colonies of Europe states. So, most of them now live in France, Italy and Germany.

Malta is one of the smallest countries in the world, situated in the South of Europe. Malta is an island state. Maltese language is a branch of semitic language family.

NATIONS OF AFRICA

Africa is the second largest continent after Eurasia. It's surrounded by Mediterranean Sea in the north, Red sea in northeast, Atlantic Ocean in the west and Indian Ocean in the east and south. An area is about 30.3 million km square. The population is approximately 1.1 billion. There are 56 countries and 2 of them are disputable. The biggest rivers in Africa are Nile, Congo and Niger. During the conquests of Africa by Europeans, the number of local population consisted of 20% of the world, but in 1960s it decreased till 8%. In 90s of the XX century there lived more than 520 million people. There are more than a thousand (by UNESCO it was estimated around 2 thousand.) languages spoken in Africa. Africa is the most multilingual continent in the world. The populations here speak not only in African languages but also in European languages. There are 4 major language families indigenous to Africa:

1. The Afroasiatic languages are a language family of about 240 languages and 285 million people widespread throughout the Horn of Africa, North Africa, the Sahel, and Southwest Asia.
2. The Nilo-Saharan language family consists of more than a hundred languages spoken by 30 million people. Nilo-Saharan languages are spoken by ethnic groups in Chad, Ethiopia, Kenya, Nigeria, Sudan, South Sudan, Uganda, and northern Tanzania.
3. The Niger-Congo language family covers much of Sub-Saharan Africa.
4. The Khoisan languages number about 50 and are spoken in Southern Africa by approximately 120,000 people. Many of the Khoisan languages are endangered. The Khoi and San

peoples are considered the original inhabitants of this part of Africa.

English, French, Spanish, German, Italian languages are also spread among the population of Africa. It's because of the protectorate period of Africa and of course it caused impacts to the language of peoples.

African culture is studied by many scholars and there is information from sources about African Renaissance period (This concept was first articulated by Cheikh Anta Diop in a series of essays at the beginning of 1946) which during this time, there took place African traditional cultural movement led by Thabo Mbeki (Thabo Mvuyelwa Mbeki is a South African politician who served 9 years as the 2nd post-apartheid President of South Africa from 14 June 1999 to 24 September 2008). It's known as Afrocentrism. Afrocentrism (also Afrocentricity) is a cultural ideology or worldview mostly limited to the United States that focuses on the history of black Africans.

There are five races in Africa according to anthropologists:

1. Black African
2. White
3. Coloured
4. Asian
5. Other/Unspecified

Except these, there are also members of transition and mixed races. There is a special race which is the mixed of Negroid with europoid raced - Ethiopian. African continent is divided into several ethnographic provinces:

1. North Africa

2. Sudan
3. Ethiopia
4. Eastern - tropic Africa
5. Western - tropic Africa
6. Southern Africa
7. Madagascar nations

In the North Africa Arabic language is a dominant language. Except this, in some areas population speak in their local languages. These areas mostly north part of Africa. In area also was spread Islam religion. Majority of Northern Africa are Muslims. They mostly live in Egypt, Libya, Algeria, Tunis, Morocco and Sudan. Except of Southern African Republic, north part of Africa is distinguished from south with its cultural, political, economical and social situation. They are better developed than other parts of continent. In North Africa are situated a lot of countries such as Algeria, Egypt, Libya, Morocco, Sudan and etc. There were developed different styles of architecture. How we know, after the Arab campaigns, Islam was spread in Africa. Soon in the XIX century Africa became a colony of European states. In the XX century there took place liberation movements. Africans began to struggle for their independence. As a result of this, there appeared new states.

Northern Africa. Egypt was one of the centers of ancient Eastern civilizations. This region had a good geographical position. Because, Northern Africa was border with Mediterranean Sea and it was a cause for wide relations with European countries. It became independent on the 28th February of 1922. Official language of state is Arab language and capital is Cairo. The number of population is approximately 80.5 million. The ethnic composition of Egypt is consisted of 91% of Arabs and also there are nubians, berbers, Beja, turks people and so on. The term Nubian describes an ethnic group that originated in modern-day Sudan and Egypt. They speak a variety of Nilo-Saharan languages in the Nubian language family. Nubian people have a long history dating back to dynastic Egypt. Nubians founded a dynasty that ruled Upper and Lower Egypt during the 8th century BC. Berbers or Amazighen are an ethnic group indigenous to North Africa. Historically, they spoke Berber languages, which together form the Berber branch of the Afro-Asiatic family. After the colonization of North Africa by France, there was spread French language among Berbers. The majority of Berbers are predominantly Sunni Muslim. The Beja speak the Beja language as a mother tongue, which belongs to the Cushitic branch of the Afro-Asiatic family. They are also Sunni Muslims. In Egypt 90% of population are Muslims, 9% are Christian-Copts and 1% other Christians. The Copts are an ethno-religious group that primarily inhabits the area of modern Egypt. Historically, they spoke the Coptic language, a direct descendant of the Demotic Egyptian that was spoken during the Roman era. The Coptic language is a focus of Coptology and remains in liturgical use, although most Copts today speak Arabic.

Sudan is located in the Eastern Africa and the capital of this republic is Khartoum. 70% of population of Sudan are consisted of arabs and also there live beja people. The official languages of Sudan are Arab and English languages. 95% of population are Sunni Muslims, but there are also christians and aboriginal religions. In the Sudan's territory live peoples who related to Afroasia, Nile - Sakhara and Niger - Kordofan language families.

Ethiopia is a Greek word and it means "country where live people whose face became black because of the sun." Ethiopia belongs to the countries which are considered as multinational and multilingual. There live Muslims, Christians and population who believe to other religions. The number of population of Ethiopia is approximately 96 million. Ethnic composition of Ethiopia is consists of Somali, tigrayans, sidama, gurage, amhara, Oromo peoples and etc. About 4.6 million Somalis live in Ethiopia, mostly they are sunni muslims and speak in somali language which is part of Cushitic branch of Afro-Asiatic language family. Tigrayans, also known as Biher-Tigrinyas speak in Tigrinya language which belongs to the Semitic branch of Afro-Asiatic language family and live in Tigray region of Ethiopia. The Sidama people of southern Ethiopia are an ethnic group whose homeland is in the Sidama zone of the southern nations of Ethiopia and majority of them protestant Christians. The Sidama preserved their cultural heritage, including their traditional religion and language until the late 1880s during the conquest by Emperor Menelik II. The Gurage people are a semitic-speaking ethnic group inhabiting Ethiopia. The languages spoken by the Gurage are known as the Gurage languages. The Amhara people are an ethnic group inhabiting the northern and central highlands of Ethiopia, particularly the Amhara Region. They speak Amharic, an Afro-Asiatic language of the Semitic branch, and are one of the Habesha peoples. The Oromo people are an ethnic group inhabiting Ethiopia and northern Kenya, with around 38 million members. Oromos speak the Oromo language as a mother tongue which is part of the Cushitic branch of the Afro-Asiatic family.

Tropical Africa. Tropical Africa is settled by peoples who speak in Bantu and Sudan languages. In Western Tropic Africa population is engaged in planting and hunting. But in Eastern Tropic Africa population is engaged in plating and cattle - breeding.

The most famous nation in African continent is **Masai**

tribe. They live in the south of Kenya (350000 - 450 000) and in the north of Tanzania (450 000 - 550 000). Although most of population of Africa developed and became more modern, they kept their all old traditional life. They speak in Masaian language. We don't know precisely their number of population. Because there is no effective documentation in this area, they haven't passports and that's why there isn't a certain statistic. Masai belongs to the Nile group of language families. They migrated from the areas near Nile to Sudan and to central and south part of Kenya after 1500 AD. They brought with themselves their domesticated cattle. Although other African tribes during this time established kingdoms and so on Masai lived traditionally. During the centuries, because of urbanization and epidemic of dream disease which was spread of a fly tsetse, population of them decreased and that's why they became weakly. The cattle are very sacred for Massais. As a legend, the god of rain - Ngai gave cattle to Massai. Because of this, there was a conflict with other tribes. They wanted to rob sacred cattle from Massai. They also have some rituals. They drank blood of cow. Modern - day Kenya is one of the places of tourism. When it firstly happened, Massais couldn't use situation and also to get money from tourism. Nowadays, they usually tried to use situations and they asked tourists to give them money and also they didn't allow taking photo of them without money and also they photoshop their pictures. Massai is considered as a symbol of Africa which against modernization. Among them there are warriors who have own tactics and so on. It's related to the ancient times. There are 2 famous Massai origin peoples: David Rudisha - olympic champion of 2012 of running, Bolaji Badedjo - actor.

South Africa. The north borders of Southern Africa are surrounded with Zambezi River. In South Africa are located countries such as Botswana, Lesotho, Namibia, Swaziland and Southern Africa. The Netherlands established the first European settlements in the middle of the XVII century in Southern Africa. Then English peoples dominated in this area. In the territory mostly were spread bushmens and Hottentots. And also there live peoples who speak in Bantu languages. Bushmens and Hottentots belong to the same anthropological type and they consisted of Koysan group. The 'Bushmen' are the oldest inhabitants of Southern Africa, where they have lived for at least 20,000 years. Their home is in the vast expanse of the Kalahari Desert. There are many different Bushmen peoples - they have no collective name for themselves, and the terms 'Bushmen', 'San', 'Basarwa' (in Botswana) and so on are used variously. Most of those which are widely understood are imposed by outsiders and have some pejorative sense; many now use and accept the term 'Bushmen'. They speak a variety of languages, all of which incorporate 'click' sounds represented in writing by symbols such as ! or /. The Bushmen are hunter-gatherers, who for thousands of years supported themselves in the desert through these skills. They hunt - mainly various kinds of antelope - but their daily diet has always consisted more of the fruits, nuts and roots which they seek out in the desert. They make their own temporary homes from wood that they gather. Many Bushmen who have been forced off their lands now live in settlements in areas that are unsuitable for hunting and gathering - they support themselves by growing some food, or by working on ranches. The Bushmen had their homelands invaded by cattle herding Bantu tribes from around 1,500 years ago, and by white colonists over the last few hundred years. From that time they faced discrimination, eviction from their ancestral lands, murder and oppression amounting to a massive though unspoken genocide, which reduced them in numbers from several million to 100,000. Today, although all suffer from a perception that their lifestyle is 'primitive' and that they need to be made to live like the majority cattle-herding tribes, specific problems vary according to where they live. In South Africa, for example, the Khomani now have most of their land rights recognised, but many other Bushman tribes have no land rights at all.

Except bushmens and Hottentots, there live zuluses too. The Zulu are the largest ethnic group in South Africa. They are well known for their beautiful brightly colored beads and baskets as well as other small carvings. The Zulu believe that they are descendents from a chief from the Congo area, and in the XVI century migrated south picking up many of the traditions and customs of the San who also inhabited South African area. During the XVII and XVIII centuries many of the most powerful chiefs made treaties and gave control of the Zulu villages to the British. This caused much conflict because the Zulu had strong patriarchal village government systems so they fought against the British but couldn't win because of the small strength they possessed. Finally, after much of the Zulu area had been given to the British the Zulu people decided as a whole that they didn't want to be under British rule and in 1879 war erupted between the British and the Zulu. Though the Zulu succeeded at first they were in 6 months conquered by the British who exiled the Zulu Kings and divided up the Zulu kingdom. In 1906 another Zulu uprising was lead and the Zulu continue to try to gain back what they consider to be their ancient kingdom. The Zulu believe in a creator god known as Nkulunkulu, but this god does not interact with humans and has no interest in everyday life. Therefore, most Zulus interact on a day to day level with the spirits. In order to interact with the spirits the Zulu must use divination to interact with the ancestors. All misfortune is a result of a evil sorcery or offended spirits, nothing just happens because of natural causes. The Zulu are practically divided in half with about 50% living in cities and engaging in domestic work and another 50% working on farms.

In African continent, there is only one developed capitalist country - South African Republic. South Africa is the 25th largest country in the world by land area and with close to 53 million people, is the world's 24th most populous nation. It is a multiethnic society encompassing a wide variety of cultures, languages, and religions. It has three capital cities:

1. Pretoria (executive)
2. Bloemfontein (judicial)
3. Cape Town (legislative)

The largest city of South Africa is Johannesburg. South Africa got independence from United Kingdom on the 31st may of 1910. South Africa has 11 official languages: Afrikaans, English, Ndebele, Northern Sotho, Sotho, Swazi, Tswana, Tsonga, Venda, Xhosa, and Zulu. The 3 most spoken first languages are Zulu (22.7%), Xhosa (16.0%), and Afrikaans (13.5%). 12 million of population speaks in Indo - European languages. The country also recognizes several unofficial languages, including Fanagalo, Khoe, Lobedu, Nama, Northern Ndebele, Phuthi, and South African Sign Language. This area is rich with resources. Majority of population believe to Christianity. There are also local religions in some area.

Madagascar people. Madagascar is one of the biggest islands in the world and it's previously known as the Malagasy Republic. It's an island country in the Indian Ocean, on the coast of Southeast Africa. The first archaeological evidence for human foraging on Madagascar dates to 2000 BC. Human settlement of Madagascar occurred between 350 BC and AD 550 by Austronesian peoples. Austronesians are various populations in Asia, Oceania and Africa that speak languages of the Austronesian family. These were joined around AD 1000 by Bantu migrants crossing the Mozambique Channel from East Africa. Other groups continued to settle on Madagascar over time, each one making lasting contributions to Malagasy cultural life. The Malagasy ethnic group is often divided into 18 or more sub-groups of which the largest are the Merina of the central highlands. In the early 19th century, most of the island was united and ruled as the Kingdom of Madagascar by a series of Merina nobles. The monarchy collapsed in 1897 when island became a colony of French empire, but on the June 26 of 1960 island gained independence. The capital of Madagascar is Antananarivo. The official languages are french and Malagasy languages. The modern language of population of Madagascar belongs to the west group of Indonesian languages. The population with their language, culture and antropological differences mostly like to the Indonesia, not Africa. The number of population is about 21 million. There are 3 kinds of tribes in Madagascar:

1. Mountain tribes - Merina people are the dominant "highlander" Malagasy ethnic group in Madagascar. Their core territory corresponds to the former Antananarivo province in the center of the island. At the beginning of the late 18th century Merina sovereigns dominated over the rest of the island. The number of Merina peoples is 5 million. They speak in Malagasy language. Malagacy language has some features of Bantu, Arab, French and English languages. The language has written literature from the 15th century and it has oral poetic traditions.
2. Coastal tribes - sakalava, betsimisaraka, antaisaka people

and etc. The Sakalava are an ethnic group of Madagascar. Their name means "people of the long valleys." They occupy the western edge of the island from Toliara in the south to Sambirano in the north. The Betsimisaraka people ("the many inseparables") are the second largest ethnic group in Madagascar after the Merina. They occupy a large stretch of the eastern seabord of Madagascar, from Mananjary in the south to Antalaha in the north. The Betsimisaraka have a long history and they also had relations with Europeans and that's why European culture influenced to their culture. They speak in several dialects of the Malagasy language, which is a branch of the Malayo-Polynesian language group derived from the Barito languages, spoken in southern Borneo. The Antesaka people are also known as Tesaka or Tesaki. They are an ethnic group of Madagascar traditionally concentrated south of Farafangana along the south-eastern coast. The Antesaka form about 5% of the population of Madagascar. They have mixed African, Arab and Malayo-Indonesian ancestry, like the western coastal Sakalava people. They traditionally have strong marriage taboos. The Antesaka typically cultivate coffee, bananas and rice and those along the coast engage in fishing. A large portion of the population has emigrated to other parts of the island for work. About 40% of emigrants between 1948 and 1958 permanently settled outside the Antesaka homeland. The group was founded by Andriamandresy - a Sakalava prince.

3. Hybrid tribes

Approximately half of the Madagascar's population practice traditional religion. There are also catholic and protestant

Christians.

NATIONS OF AMERICA

America or The Americas is the two continents taken together - North America and South America. Along with their associated islands, they cover 42.5 km square that 8% of Earth's total surface area and 28.4% of its land area. The population is over 1 billion, with over 65% of them living in one of the three most populous countries (USA, Brazil, Mexico). Commonly, America does not include to the territory where humans were appeared. But there are some legends which show that may be here is the area of the initial humans. But this is not exact information and it may be the thoughts and imagines of the humans of the American continent for the creation of world. According to some sources, the American continent was settled by the modern physical-typed humans who are called as "Homo Sapiens". The cultural level of the population of the New World complies with the Mesolithic or the Last Neolithic culture of Europe. Geologically, initial settlement of humans in America dates back to the end of the Ice Age, more exactly, 40 000 years ago. Most of the Local population of America anthropologically is closer with the mongoloids. They have also some features of Australoid and it proves a group of population who had such racial features settled in America too. At the same time, both of the population groups came here just with the help of the Bering Strait.

The American explorer M. Suadesh wrote that indigenous nations of America were speaking in the different dialects of the common language even 15 000-20 000 years ago. After the third discovery of America by the Europeans it was determined that there are more than 2200 indian languages.

The history of the discovery and settlement of America is divided into 2 periods. The first period began approximately 40 000 years ago and lasted till the end of the XV century AD. The second period began from the Great Geographical Discoveries which are related with the name of Ch. Columbus and lasted more than 4 centuries.

A. Crober, F. Boas, and E. Sepir played great roles in the researches of the mutual relations of the American languages. Currently, the language families of the local peoples of America are Escimos-aleut, Penuti, Sockie-Mayya, Quechua, Aymara, Caribian, Je (Jes), Algonckin-Vackash, Na-dene, Siu-khoca, Tano-yuto-astec, Macrootomi, Chibcha, Araican, Aravac, Tupi-quarani, Chon language families. It was determined that there are 58 language groups in America. After the discovery of the American continent, Spaniards and Portugueses in the South and the English, the French and particularly Holland in the North realized colonialist policy. During the colonialist period, thousands of local population were killed by them and a lot of black people or Negros were resettled here from the African continent. Nowadays, the number of indians is relatively higher in Latin America. Indian paeople mostly live in Mexico, Peru and Guatemala. The common number of the indians is 36.5 million. Negros settled mostly in USA. Here, the number of Negros is about 29 million.

In the southern end of the South America and near the Antarctica there are situated the islands of the Land of Fire. The population settled here consists of 3 indian groups: Ona, Alacalouf and Yagan. These clan groups are different from one-another for their languages and cultures. Currently, the number of the population belonged to these clans has decreased.

When European colonizers reached the shores of New World, they encountered indigenous people, possessing rich and sophisticated culture. Objective study of the period suggests rude attitude of colonizers, who melted local jewelry into gold bars and burned ancient writings.

The fact that indigenous people of North America were backwards compared to European nations and had prehistoric society offered an incentive to many ethnographers to reconstruct development of ancient societies on the basis of specific cultures of North America. As example, L. H. Morgan formulated the theory on the evolution of family. His most influential work "Ancient History" clarifies many issues regarding the evolution of society and covers growth of such ideas as intelligence, government, family and property. It should be noted that his theory on family is currently abandoned.

For systematic purposes modern ethnography uses cultural areas and farming habitats. However this type of classification usually contradicts with linguistic division. For example, although Athabaskan language family mostly occupies population of Alaska, the Yukon and Northwest territories, people of Navajo also speak this language in the South West region.

Well-developed local nations. There have been living also highly-cultured local peoples in the Central and South America. The Mayan, Aztec and Inca civilizations are the highest local civilizations or cultures of these areas since the ancient times. **The Mayan civilization** has been spread widely in Guatemala, Belize, Salvador, Honduras and Mexico. The Mayans are the ancient people who are known in history for their alphabet, art, architecture, math and astronomic system. It is assumed that the Mayan culture emerged beginning from 2000 BC and this culture was destroyed intensively after the coming of Spanish colonists in the 16-th century AD. But, the remains of the Mayan culture and the successors of the ancient Mayan people still exist. This people built stone buildings during the ancient times and some parts of these buildings are in use nowadays. Some of their settlements have been included to the World Heritage Site of UNESCO. More than 1000 settlements have been found till now which belong to the Mayan culture. The main cities are Palencke, Copan, Ushmal, Tical, Bonampac, Chichen-Itsa, Yashchilan, Piedras-Negras, El-Bayul, Labna, Sayil and etc. Historically,these cities were ruled by the kingdoms of Baacul, Mutul and Canul. The ancient epitaph of the Mayan people which was found out by archaeologists is in the Oaxaca state of Mexico nowadays and it belongs to 700 AD. The Mayan calendar was used from the other peoples in the Central America too.

The Mayan alphabet was in hieroglyph system. But, Diego de Landa who had written the first scientific book in the Mayan writing system thought that the Mayan alphabet is alike with the Latin alphabet and every symbol is equal to one letter. Of course, these were not right at all. Yuri V. C. was the first scientist who decoded the Mayan hieroglyphs. Today, the Mayans more than 6 million live in Yucatan peninsula, Belize, Guatemala and Honduras. Their old language – the Mayan language belongs to the Uto-Aztecan language family. The

Yucatan Mayans have a special, traditional clothing style which is one of the differences of them. Their religion has been formed in a synthesis of catholic Christianity with the traditional Mayan religion.

The traditional religion of the Mayans is polytheistic. There was an interesting ritual custom among this people so-called "to shed blood" which was one of the traditions of most of the other peoples in the world too. We can see the evidences of this ritual in the pictures of ceramics which were found from the excavations. The process of the shedding blood was realizing in different ways. For example, firstly, the victim was drowned in water, then the beating heart of the victim was taken with the method of cutting of chest with sharp knives which were made from volcanic stones and at least, this heart was thrown to the large underground water-supply so-called "Senot". Beside this method, there were other methods of blood-shedding. According to the beliefs of the Mayans, blood was considered as a symbol of human's soul and the source of human's energy.

Aztecs. The Aztec civilization or the Aztec culture has been spread in Mexico, mostly. This civilization was formed by the Aztec people who were the certain groups of central Mexico and they spoke the Nahuatl language. This language belongs to the south branch of the Uto-Aztecan language family and to a large group of Indian languages which also include the languages spoken by the Comanche, Pima, Shoshone and other tribes of the western part of the North America. It is also used in Salvador by the Nahuas. In the Nahuatl language, the words are used like this: in English "tomato" and in Nahuatl "tomatl", "chocolate" – "xocolatl", "avocados" – "ahuacatl" and etc.

The Aztecs were considered a Pre-Columbian Mesoamerican people of central Mexico in the XIV-XVI centuries too. Also, the word "Aztec" comes from this language which means "people from Aztlan". There is a legend that Aztlan was a mythological place or island meaning White Place-Place of Herons". Often the term "Aztec" is referred to the inhabitants of the Tenochtitlan city. There is an empire in history, which is directly related to the Aztecs and it was called as "Aztec Empire". The Tenochtitlan city was a capital and the largest city of the Aztec empire and it was built on raised island in Lake Texcoco. The empire was made from 2 principal allied city-states, the Acolhuas of Texcoco and the Tepanecs of Tlacopan who together with Mexico formed the Aztec Triple Alliance. The center of the Aztec civilization was the Valley of Mexico. This territory is a huge, oval basin about 7 500 feet above sea level. Commonly, the Aztecs were a relatively unknown people who came into the Valley of Mexico between 12-13-th centuries and they reached to the greatest power in the Americas by the time the Spaniards arrived in the 16-th century. Scientists reported that not many things we know about the earliest Aztecs. Because, they did not have written records. Their history was passed on by word of mouth from one generation to the next.

The Aztecs felt they were the "chosen people" of Huitzilopochtli. The Aztecs believed Huitzilopochtli who was their War God and the God of the Sun, was their protector and he chose this people for their promised land. They worshiped him daily in the Main Temple. The Aztecs were polytheistic, believing in many gods. Prophecies were a part of the ancient Aztec religion. Many scholars today believe that the Aztec people thought that the conqueror Cortes was their God-Hero Quetzalcoatl, who had been banished. The more educated upper class shared this belief is questionable. Also, the Aztecs believed in reincarnation. Some would eventually be reincarnated as birds or butterflies or eventually humans. In the other way, they thought that humans fell into the long journey after the death and they had to pass through the 9 levels of the underworld. In the end they would live in the darkness. Because of this, the Aztec people buried the dead in a squatting position, with items that would help them in their journey.

The Aztecs of Tenochtitlan though it necessary to nourish the deities with human hearts, because if not, then the sun would not come up daily, or there would be an enormous drought. The people mostly used prisoners of war for their sacrifices. The main place of sacrifice was the Great Pyramid. It had 114 steps and added to the magnificent beauty of the city. The Plaza was in the dead center of the city, and was whitewashed. It had no litter whatsoever, and great walls surrounding it. The Plaza and all of these structures make the center look like a thing of beauty.

Aztec philosophy saw the concept of Teotl as a fundamental unity that underlies the entire universe. Teotl is all things. Even things in opposite- light and dark, life and death were seen as expressions of the same unity, teotl. The belief in a unity with dualistic expressions compares with similar dialectical monist ideas in both Western and Eastern philosophies.

Prior to the fall of the Aztec, the Aztec people had a stable economy driven by a successful trade market. The markets which were located in the center of many communities were well-organized and diverse in goods, as noted by the Spanish conquistadors upon their arrival. The regional merchants known as "tlanecuilo" tended to barter utilitarian items and foodstuffs which included gold, silver and other precious stones, cloth, cotton, animal skins, both agriculture and wild game and woodwork. The most of the merchants became wealthier like the nobles because of the rise of the trade.

The Aztecs were a magnificent race of people who preserved Tenochtitlan for over 200 years. The Aztecs had a lot of players, musicians, poets and acrobats. The society of them was divided into 3 classes: slaves, commoners, and nobility. In the context of the family, men and women played distinct roles. Aztec women married about 16. At school, boys were taught arts and crafts and girls were taught to cook and other necessities to raise a family.

There are books so called "Aztec codices" written by pre-Columbian and colonial-era Aztecs. These codices provide some of the best primary sources for Aztec culture. The pre-Columbian codices differ from European codices in that they are largely pictorial. They were not meant to symbolize spoken or written narratives. The colonial era codices not only contain Aztec pictograms, but also Classical Nahuatl (in the Latin alphabet), Spanish and occasionally Latin. Scholars now have access to a body of around 500 colonial-era codices.

The principal food of the Aztecs was a thin cornmeal pancake called a tlaxcalli. It is called in Spanish "tortilla". This people have been credited with the discovery of chocolate. They made chocolate from the fruit of the cacao tree and used it as a flavoring and as an ingredient in various beverages and kinds of confectionery. Cortes brought cacao beans to Spain and new formula of drink was made from chocolate, which was heated with added sweeteners.

Today's Aztecs are the Mexicans. They are interested in education beginning from the ancient times. The education of girls, boys and young people was valuable for them even during the middle ages. It's nearly 500 years since Cortes overthrew Tenochtitlan but you can still find Aztecs in every walk of life doing the same kind of things but not sacrifice bit. In 1982 an estimated 1 million people were of Aztec descent. The Aztec religion is still maintained. But, Christianity has also been spread among them, although a religious movement so-called "Mexicanista" happened in Mexico in the XX century. This movement called for a return to the spirituality of the Aztecs. It is argued that, with this return, Mexico will become the next center of power. This religious movement mixes Mesoamerican cults with indian esoterism. The Mexicanista movement reached the peak of its popularity in the 1990s. It was also called as a movement of Neopaganism. Most of the Aztecs are credited with domestication of the subspecies of Wild turkey, Meleagris gallopavo, which is native to this region. They grow corn, chili peppers, squash, tomatoes, beans, and other kinds of food.

Incas. Inca civilization belongs to the countries of the Andean mountains such as Peru, Chili, Columbia and Ecuador.

It flourished in ancient Peru between 1400 b. c and 1533 AD and the Inca Empire eventually extended across western South America from Quito in the north to Santiago in the south, making it the largest empire ever seen in the Americas and the largest in the world at that time. Undaunted by the often harsh Andean environment, the Incas conquered people and exploited landscapes in such diverse settings as plains, mountains, deserts and tropical jungle. Famed for their unique art and architecture they constructed finely-built and imposing buildings wherever they conquered and their spectacular adaptation of natural landscapes with terracing, highways and mountaintop settlements continues to impress modern visitors at such world famous sites as Machu Picchu.

As the other American peoples, the Incas history is difficult to learn exactly. Mainly, scholars reveal their history and early life with the help of the myths which were created by them. According to legend, in the beginning, the creator God Viracocha came out of the Pacific Ocean and when he arrived at Lake Titicaca, he created the sun and all ethnic groups. These first people were buried by the God and only later they emerged from springs and rocks (sacred Pacarinas) back into the world. The Incas specifically were brought into existence at Tiwanaku (Tiahuanaco) from the Sun God Inti, hence, they regarded themselves as the chosen few the "Children of the Sun" and Inca ruler was Inti's representative and embodiment on Earth. In another version of the creation myth, the first Incas came from a sacred cave known as "Tampu Toqo" or "The House of Windows", which was located at Pacariqtambo, the "Inn of Dawn", south of Cuzco. The first pair of humans were Manco Capac (or Manqo Qhapaq) and his sister (also his wife) Mama Oqllu (or Ocllo). Three more brother-sister siblings were born and the group set off together to found their civilization. Defeating the Chanca people with the help of stone warriors (pururaucas), the first Incas finally settled in the Valley of Cuzco and Manco Capac, throwing a golden rod into the ground, established what would become the Inca capital, Cuzco.

The Inca Empire had good military forces for that time. The socio-economic and political situation was stabilized. For tax purposes censuses were taken and populations divided up into groups based on multiples of ten. Inca mathematics was almost identical to the system we use today. As there was no currency in the Inca world, taxes were paid in kind-usually foodstuffs, precious metals, textiles, exotic feathers, dyes and spondylus shell - but also in laborers who could be shifted about the empire to be used where they were most needed known as mit'a service. Agricultural land and herds were divided into 3 parts: production for the state religion and the Gods, for the Inca ruler and for the farmers own use.

The Inca capital of Cuzco was the religious and administrative centre of the empire and had a population of up to 150 000 at its peak. Dominated by the sacred gold-covered and emerald-studded Coricancha complex (or Temple of the Sun), its greatest buildings were credited to Pachacuti. Most splendid were the temples built in honor of Inti and Mama Kilya - the former was lined with 7002 kg sheets of beaten gold, the latter with silver. The whole capital was laid out in the form of a puma with the imperial metropolis of Pumachupan forming the tail and the temple complex of Sacsayhuaman (or Saqsawaman) forming the head.

Incorporating vast plazas, parklands, shrines, fountains and canals, the splendor of Inca Cuzco now, unfortunately, survives only in the eye-witness accounts of the first Europeans who marveled at its architecture and riches.

Inca rulers made regular pilgrimages to Tiwanaku and the islands of the lake, where 2 shrines were built to Inti - the Sun God and supreme Inca deity, and the Moon Goddess Mama Kilya. Also in the Coricancha complex at Cuzco, these deities were represented by large precious metal artworks which were attended and worshipped by priests and priestesses led by the second most important person after the king: the High Priest of the Sun (Willaq Umu). Thus, the religion of the Inca was preoccupied with controlling the natural world and avoiding such disasters as earthquake, floods and drought which inevitably brought about the natural cycle of change, the turning over of time involving death and renewal which the Inca called "pachakuti". The most sacred Inca site was Pachacamac, a temple city built in honor of the God with the same name, who created humans, plants, and was responsible for earthquakes. Shamans were another important part of Inca religion and were active in every settlement. Cuzco had 475, the most important being the yacarca, the personal advisor to the ruler. To give sacrifices from animals, humans including children were for the gods and the good health of the king. The pouring of libations, either water or "chicha" beer was also an important part of Inca religious ceremonies. The Incas believed in 3 worlds: the world above "Wiracocha", the world we live on "Pacha Mama" and the world below or "underworld".

The architecture of the Incas was in high level for that time. One of the most common buildings was the ubiquitous one-room storage warehouse the "qollqa". Built in stone and well-ventilated they were either round or stored maize or square for potatoes and tubers. The "kallanka" was a very large hall used for community gatherings. "Kancha"- a group of small single room and rectangular buildings (wasi and masma) with thatched roofs built around a courtyard enclosed by a high wall was a typical architectural feature of Inca towns and the idea was exported to conquered regions.

The Incas produced textiles, ceramics and metal sculpture technically superior to any previous Andean culture and this was competitive like the Moche civilization.

Inca had a very different way of writing and speaking. Many people believe that they used a technique called "Quipu" or "Khipu" which is the process of putting knots in a long cord of rope or string. The language that the Inca spoke was known as "Quechua". The Quechua language is still used today and includes to the Quechuan language family. This is the official language of Peru, Bolivia and Ecuador in modern days.

The Inca philosophy of today is influenced by several different elements. It is the combination of the ancient South American Inca Gods - Wiracocha and Pacha Mama, together with Jesus Christ whose ministry was introduced to South America by the Catholic Church. Commonly, the Inca religion is divided into these periods: Creation, The coming of Jesus Christ, Holy Spirit current period.

The official language of most of the countries in the South America is the Spanish language and most of the population speaks in this language. There are also Gypsies in the Latin American countries. But in Brazil, the official language is the Portuguese language. In Peru, the official languages are the Spanish language and also Quechuan languages. The ancient local religions still remain in some areas. The local religions have been spread largely in the central parts of the South America. Most of the population believe in Christianity.

Commonly, the South America consists of 12 independent and 3 dependent states. 2 of the dependent states are island states. The largest country of the South Americais Brazil and the smallest is Suriname. The most of the population of Brazil is white people (47.73 percent) and the black people are 7.61 percent). Brazil is famous for its interesting and amazing carnivals and also for the great organizations of sports games. Most of the population of Suriname is the East Indian people (27.4 percent) and the others are mixed peoples. Suriname has been under the power of the Netherlands till 1975. Now, the official language is Dutch and the other principal language is Sranan in Suriname.

Arctic hunters and fishermen. Nowadays, there are two major groups of people in Alaska: Yupik and Inupiat. In Canada the word the "Eskimo" is considered derogatory and term "Inuit" is used instead. By the way, not all arctic people ethnically are Inupiat origin. The latter group is referred to as the Eskimo.

Eskimo people occupied coastline of Alaska, Labrador peninsula and Greenland. Nowadays, the term "Eskimo" is regarded as derogatory in Canada, and the word "Innuit" is preferred. Meat of seal, walrus and whales i.e. sea mammals; hunting of land mammals; and fishing was a primary meaning of substance for Eskimo groups. Fat of sea mammals was used for illumination purposes, while skin was used for clothing. Cooking wasn't popular among Eskimos for practical reasons, which included better preservation of vital nutrients in raw meat and small oil reservations.

Labor tools of copper are rare, as Eskimo groups could get it only through natural exchange with Northern neighbors. Stone and bones were used a lot wider. Wale ribs were used for constructions of dwellings. The wood was valued as well. Toggling harpoon was one of the sophisticated tools for sea hunting. Its main difference from normal harpoon was detachable head, which immediately twisted horizontally once the animal is wounded. This detachable head was connected with a string with the rest of harpoon and made it difficult to pull off for the animal. One of these tools was excavated in Labrador.

Depending on natural conditions, the Eskimos could prefer individual or group hunting. Traditional kayak and umiak were used for sea transportation. As kayak was smaller in size and was intended for 1-2 individuals, it was used in hunting. Although local women were involved in collection of berries during polar summer, Eskimos people didn't have plant based diet. Instead these people had contents of the herbivores animals as traditional meal.

Some Eskimo tribes had to leave their dwellings in search for prey. For land transportation strong sled dogs were essential and in the result of Gold Rush late 1800 and early

1900 were called "Era of the Sled Dog". The Eskimos used dugouts mostly in winter. The Inughuit (formerly "Polar Eskimos") are famous for constructing their dwellings of snow bricks in the form of hemisphere. It appears that such dwellings were covered with skins from the inside as well as heated with animal fat burning. Tents covered with skin and bark also appear in this period.

The Eskimos used in groups of 2-3 families. It seems like at the time of European colonization the agnatic kinship started to form. Eskimos had weak links between groups mentioned above as each group needed to occupy vast territories to get access to the meanings of substance. The Eskimos did believe in the power of nature over people and worshiped the "goddess of the sea". Shamans were prominent members of the society.

Sedentary tribes of North-Western coastline. The coastline of Pacific Ocean is inhabited by Haida, Tsimshian, Nuu-chah-nulth (formerly Nutka), Tlingit, Kwakiutl and Salish peoples. Most of them lived in the relatively small territories stretching from Canadian Rockies to the Columbia River and Yakutat. Although these groups inherited different languages, their lifestyle provided mostly equal natural circumstances for fishing to thrive. Hunting of mammals and gathering was second to the fishing, but was of vital importance because of necessity in skins and meat.

Trapping, tackles and harpoons were essential during fishing. The boats usually consisted of a solid piece of wood. Interestingly enough, people of the region discovered that Eulachon species (better known as "Candle Fish") is a fish with a great amount of body fat, so when dried and fired up it can be used as a candle. Wild sheep and goats were trapped into yards and then clipped to get wool for clothing.

Such abundance of resources brought to the rapid development of social inequality and more importantly slavery much earlier than the arrival of first Europeans to the continent. Wars maintained stable thread of new slaves through subjugation of neighboring tribe members. However, the slavery was on its early stages, as the society of these people was classified as prehistoric.

The tribes were divided into phratries, which in turn were divided into genes. This term was invented by L.H. Morgan, who noted similarity of Greek phratries, mentioned by Homer during Dark Ages, and society structure of the Tlingit tribe of Northern America, which also preserved tradition of matrilineal inheritance of property. The members of one gene used to believe in common animal ancestor. The belief of common ancestor was important, as not only gene, but also the whole phratry usually was named after this totemic creature. Totems were usually found in front of the dwellings.

Mostly, fishermen of North-Western America lived in two—storey wooden houses. Such residences are regarded as patrilocal, because after marriage the couple moved to the husband's home.

As we mentioned before, people of the region lived in abundance of food resources. The leaders of the communities started to use surplus of resources for trade with other tribes, which resulted in accumulation of treasures in their hands. In such circumstances, Tlingit and Haida groups practiced a special feast of Potlach on major occasions. The word "Potlach" is translated as to "give away" or gift from the language of Nuu-chah-nulth people. Potlach was also a significant indicator of the wealth and power of the leader, as he voluntarily shared his wealth with his people and sometimes killed his slaves. Shamans were responsible for religious ceremonies. Totemism served as the basis for religious beliefs of North-Western America tribes.

The tribes of forest hunters. Forest regions of modern day Canada, inland of Alaska and Northern territories of USA became home for many hunting-gatherer tribes. Most of the peoples speak Algonquin language. These peoples are from Ojibwe, Naskapi, Kree speak.

For food these groups relied on the meat of Reindeer, also known as Caribou, as well as Moose and other taiga animals. Some people were involved in gathering of berries, fruits and roots in the forests. Although bow was used a primary weapon, hunters also used clubs, knifes and spears. The heads of arrows and spears were made of bones or stone.

The dominance of hunting among daily activities made these people keep semi-nomadic lifestyle in search of prey. Hunters covered their conical shelters with animal skins and bark. The fire was used to heat such dwelling a hole for air circulation in the roof. On the other hand, tribes of Alaska preferred dugouts.

Most of the clothing was made of animal skin. The skin of deer after processing was. Males and females wore long shirts. Moccasins made a steady skin were used by hunters. All clothing featured sophisticated ornaments with different kinds of skins and quills of porcupine. Birch bark was not only an important building material for canoes and other boats, but also was a popular and accessible labor tool material.

System of social relations was based on tribal community, but the hunting lifestyle brought some special features to such system. The community was divided into small groups of several families, which together moved from one place to another. The composition of such group was unstable, especially males joined and left such groups pretty often. These groups had traditional places for meetings, exchange of the goods and religious rituals. Each group had it own patron totem, while each individual also worshiped particular spirit. These people believed in magic and shared many beliefs in bears with peoples of Siberia.

Forest hunters established contacts with European invaders very early. In the result, fur trade gradually emerged as the main daily activity of these peoples and hunting lost its position. The rise of exchange with factory owners brought significant changes inside hunting society. The role of man raised, monogamy started to become more and more popular. But the main consequence was the emergence of social inequality. We have to bear in mind, that colonizers introduced prehistoric hunters to steel clamps and firearms. Modern tools ruined the former tribal society with alliances of different families, with the rising role of each individual family. Also cooperation during hunting was no longer needed.

Hunting tribes of prairies. Prairies are the habitats, occupying territories from Mississippi river on the east till the Canadian Rockies in the west. These territories didn't have many settlers until colonization, but under the pressure of invaders many tribes from eastern parts and Mississippi basin started to move to the region. It resulted in big language diversity in this region with Algonquin language speakers such as Arapaho and Cheyenne. Another major group was Caddo. These people shared many cultural similarities.

People of prairies relied on hunting of great herds of bisons. Literature created the image for hunter of prairies as of cavalry man with horse. However, the only domesticated animal in New World before the arrival of colonizers was a dog, which accompanied a hunter. Bow and arrows, a lot fewer spears was used as a weapon during hunting of mighty bisons. Cooperation was an important factor during hunting. In order to move closer for an attack distance hunters frequently used skins, adopting the image of wolf, other predators or the bisons themselves. Sometimes herds of bisons were forced to move towards dead ends. Just like forest hunters, these people adopted individual hunting after the arrival of foreigners. Hunting on foot was forgotten on favor to equestrian hunting.

Hunters weren't aware of metals, so all tools were made of bones and stone. As previously sedentary tribes adopted nomadic lifestyle, these people lost their knowledge about pottery. Tipi was a typical tent made of bison skin used by groups of prairies. Each family had its individual tipi. In most cases such tents were located in the form of circle with the tipi of Tribe Assemblies in the middle. The hunting season lasted the whole summer.

All property inside the tribe except the teams of horses was passed from generation to generation with matrilineal inheritance. With the development of horse-breeding the social differentiation deepened as well. Some poor individuals were hired by wealthier families for training of horses. The practice of regular attacks on the neighboring tribes with the idea of seizure property of other tribes spread quickly. With the rise of internal struggles military works also started to develop. The tribesman started to elect famous and experienced warriors to the position of tribal chiefs.

Such a rapid social development brought religious life to the next level. Indigenous people started to explore new forms of fart covering their formerly nomadic style pottery with sophisticated ornaments. They even had a calendars, cuneiform script and notes on the main events of the year.

People started to worship animals and totemism was left as a tradition of the dark past. In 1830s first colonizers arrived in the region of prairies. These people didn't care of the extinction of bisons, as they only valued the skins. In the result thousands of bisons were destroyed till 1881, when the last bizon was shot. An entire tribes of indigenous people were destroyed.

Nations of California. Indigenous people of California are divided into following language groups: Hokan, Penutian, Algonquin, Shoshone. Majority of the individuals was engaged in fishing, hunting and gathering. These tribes successfully adapted to the climatic conditions of the region and developed their gathering skills as well as special tools at the highest level. These people used corns of some oak types, seeds of wild rice and oats after strong processing for food.

Like many other people of Northern America, people of California were true nomads and newer practiced sedentary lifestyle. Most of the time people used easily mountable tents for living. In warm times of the year children didn't wear any clothes and were mostly nude. On the other hand, males used to wear loincloth and females had skirts. In cold times they used to cover their shoulders with pieces of skin.

People of California were in the process of transition from matrilineal to patrilineal kinship. Not only labor tools and territories were in community property, but also all prey and catch. The chief of the tribe was traditionally elected. In 1848 after gold mines were discovered in the region, many people came to these territories. Most of the population lost its territories and was destroyed as backward barbarians.

Land of Fire inhabitants. Land of fire archipelago situated in South American continent and it includes 40 islands. The most of archipelago belongs to Chile and there is Isla-Grande which is divided between Chile and Argentina. Firstly, it was found by Ferdinand Magellan during his world trip in 20s of 16th century. But later it was also researched by James Cook. There are 3 tribes: Yaghan, Ona and Alakaluph. These clan groups are distinguished from each other with their languages and cultures. Yaghan people talk in yaman language. In the 19th century the number of population was 3000, but now it is about 1690. 60 of them speak in yaman language and others in spanish. Mainly they are engaged in fishery and they use bows and arrows for this. The territory of Land of Fire inhabitants is surrounded by water and that's why there is good agriculture. They use also boats. After the discovery age, they were attacked and local population was killed. Today the fewest number of them still exist.

NATIONS OF AUSTRALIA AND OCEANIA

The area of Australia is 7.7 mln. sq.km which discovered by Europeans as the world's 5th continent. The area of Oceania is 1.3 mln. sq.km. Geologically, the Australia is the world's oldest continent. The highest peak is '"Mount Kosciuszko" which located in the east of mainland and the height from sea level is 2200 meter.

Depending on location of Australia in tropical and subtropical zone the fauna is poor here. This Mainland tectonically is considered as a very stable region. Many scientists mention various interpretations about population of this region and they try to make research about the date of settlement of these places. During last 20-25 years learning this problem built on the scientific foundation based on ethno-linguistic analysis of existing languages and archaeological excavation in the region. Regarding to these researches it's clear that Australia and New Guinea settled in this place.

Nations of Australia and Tasmania. The local residents of this mainland settled there 40 thousand years ago. The number of local aborigines was over 300 thousands when the English people came here. Most of the local residents were settled in separate settlements called reservation. They are not allowed close to the high culture.

Anthropologically, Australians, australo – represents small Australian race which included in a big nigger race. The people from this race have dark brown skin, black wavy hair, thick beard and mustache, broad noses, thick lips. The size of their height is average, oblong heads and prongatik faces.

The languages of Australia are colorful. The language of local Australians has some hundred years. But last assimilation process put down the number of this up to 200. Nowadays, the official language of Australia and New Zealand is English and the legislatures of these countries are subject to U.K.

Hunting is very famous in Australia. The most precious animal for them was kangaroo and other animals. Although some Australians have not permenant place to live, in the south east and west regions of mainland there are too many places to live. It has been affected natural conditions as well. So besides the emphasized places most of the other territories locating in tropical climate zone, the desert conditions were reducing the living conditions of population.

Australians have been using ships as transportation. The Australians has their strange sound national music. They like to dance under this music. The dances which called Korrobori were performed collectively. Among the religious outlook of Australians; amimizm, fetishizm, tetemizm, magia were widespread. Most famous was totemizm. But after coming Europians the Christianity was wide spread and now most of the people in Australia are christians. Facing the horrible atrocities Tasmanians were 20 thousand people in the nineteenth century. But Europeans didn't give any chance to live the Tasmanians. Last Tasmanian William Lanne dead in 1905. Tasmanians were mostly differing from Australians. They were in a much smaller size and had brown skins. They historically were in the same origin and that's why there were very large similarities in both languages. They were engaged in hunting as well as Australians do. Nowadays, Tasmanian Island is in the territory of Australia and official language is English. English speaking peoples are christians.

Nations of Oceania. The cultural development rate was different. Here the language of society and anthropological structure was also different. The population of Oceania is divided into these groups:

1. Papuas
2. Melanesia nations
3. Polynesia nations
4. Micronesia nations

Papuas live in New Guinea. New Guinean island is the second big island in the world after Greenland. The area of island is 785 thousand sq.km. In the area which called Papuasia live 750 ethnos and 572 of those are Papuas. The largest papuas ethnic group includes: enga, chimby, gagen, kamano, xuli etc.

Most of the papuas live in villages now. Main meals are made from vegetables. The generations were calculated on father's generation line. Totemism and Magia was the most used religion among Papuas.

200 ethnos live in Melanesia. Most of them speak Austronesia languages (600 000) and papuas language (70 000). Anthropologically, local society which included Australian race belongs to a race of tiny Melanesia. Languages are included to Malai – Polinesia languages. The main professions here are fishing, hunting, and farming. Melanesia villages are circular, mansions systems retail plan places. The

highest social structure in Melanesia was in Fiji archipelago. Belief in supernatural forces are widely spread.

There were beliefs to magia, animizm, totemizm so on. The Height of Polinesians 170 – 173 cm and they have dark skins and loose wavy hair. Their language belongs to Malay – Polinesia languages. The largest ethnic groups are maories, samoans, hawaiis and taitis. They are skillful craftsman. Their religion is similar with other Oceania nations. They pay too much attention to music and dance as well. Aborigines living on the island Easter of Polynesia were their own culture. It understood that they used hieroglyphics too.

There lived people in 96 islands of 2140 which belong to Micronesia. 190 thousand local ethnos live in Micronesia. Their language is part of Malay - Polinesia language family. Micronesia is divided into 2 ethnografic region:

1. West Micronesia
2. South Micronesia

Houses were built on the stone pillar. The main labor tools were stone knives, spears, bow and arrow. Fishing was popular. Weaving was wide spread. In the central and east. Micronesia people was divided into two casts:

1. The genetically nobles
2. Ordinary people called as kayur

Political Geography. Australia and Oceania's history and development have been shaped by its political geography. Political geography is the internal and external relationships between its various governments, citizens and territories. The European colonization of Australia and Oceania defined the continent's early political geography. Exploration began in the 16th century when Portuguese explorer Ferdinand Magellan landed on the Mariana Islands. European colonization was fueled by a desire to defend nationalist pride, increase trade opportunities and spread the Christian faith. England, France, Germany and Spain became the most important colonial powers in the region. Today, many countries, especially Australia, New Zealand, and New Caledonia have majority European populations and a strong European culture. English is the dominant language throughout most of the continent.

Indigenous populations were treated harshly during the colonial period. European powers claimed Australia and Oceania's lands as their own because they considered them as terra nullius or a "no man's land" inhabited by heathen natives. Colonizers implemented their own systems of governance, land management and trade. These efforts had several consequences that continue to affect indigenous groups and their cultural systems today.

Over the last half-decade, Australia and Oceania's indigenous groups have fought to extend their political rights and cultural significance in their countries. New Zealand's Maori and Aboriginal Australians are the main drivers of this movement. The Maori Party was established in 2004 to represent the rights of the Maori in New Zealand. The party's achievements for the Maori people are numerous. The party founded the Maori Economic Task force to increase economic opportunity, secured a multi-million dollar economic package for environmental initiatives and created a yearly fund of $5 million to help Maori health providers develop culturally sensitive programs.

The Maori Party is also working to incorporate the Treaty of Waitangi with New Zealand's constitution. Signed in 1840, the Treaty of Waitangi recognized Maori land and property ownership and gave Maori the same rights as the British. The treaty, however, was never truly enforced and the Maori suffered from mistreatment and discrimination. Today, the Maori Party is looking to legitimize the Treaty of Waitangi in order to claim lands lost during colonization.

Aboriginal Australians, much like the Maori, can be defined as a marginalized population or a group of people who are treated as less significant than the majority population. Aborigines suffer from disproportionately high rates of disease, imprisonment and unemployment. Aborigines' life expectancy is about 18 to 19 years less than non-indigenous people. Aborigines have a tense relationship with their home country. In 2007, the Northern Territory National Emergency Response, a federal program was created to address concerns about Aboriginal communities in Australia's isolated Northern Territory. The program put sanctions on several Aboriginal communities that were charged with child abuse. Sanctions included restrictions on the purchase of alcohol and access to pornography. These sanctions have been condemned as racist by the United Nations.

The government of Australia is working to resolve these tensions. In 2010, Ken Wyatt became the first Aboriginal Australian elected to the Australian House of Representatives. In 2008, former Prime Minister Kevin Rudd issued a public apology to members of the "Stolen Generations." The Stolen Generations were Aboriginal children taken from their families and raised under European supervision in group homes. This policy began in 1869 and officially ended in 1969.

Language of Australia. There are an estimated 150 - 650 Australian languages. While this is true we have found that most linguists settle around 250. Yallop presents the most concise breakdown of those groups. Of those 250 languages only 5 have more than 1,000 speakers today, 10 have 500-1,000 speakers, 10 have 250-500 speakers, 45 have 50-250 speakers, 130 have less than 50 speakers but are not limited in use and 50 have become extinct. (As may be apparent those that have less than 50 speakers are also on their way to extinction. Many of them are only spoken by the very old. There are currently programs being implemented to preserve these languages among the young.) These languages all fall under the heading of proto-Australian.

Tasmanian language group consisted of five dialects that have been extinct since the early twentieth century.

Historical Cultures. Indigenous cultures shaped and were shaped by the geography of Australia and Oceania. Polynesian culture, for example, developed as Southeast Asian sailors explored the South Pacific. This seafaring culture developed almost entirely from its geography.

Beginning about 1500 BCE, sailors began moving east from the island of New Guinea. The farther they traveled, the more advanced their navigation became. Polynesians developed large, double-hulled vessels called outrigger canoes. Outrigger canoes could sail very quickly across the Pacific, but they could also be easily maneuvered and paddled in rough weather. Along with outrigger canoes, historic Polynesian culture relied on a sophisticated navigation system based on observations of the stars, ocean swells and the flight patterns of birds.

Polynesians were able to domesticate plants and animals and transport them to islands that lacked native flora and fauna. This allowed Polynesians to establish stable, permanent communities throughout the islands of the South Pacific. By 1000 CE, these seafarers had colonized the islands of Melanesia, Micronesia, and Polynesia. In the process, they established a unique, ocean-oriented culture that persists today. Indigenous cultures of Australia and Oceania also changed the environments in which they lived. As they explored the South Pacific, Polynesians brought agriculture to isolated islands, for example. In another example, the Maori had a significant impact on New Zealand's forests and fauna. Between the XIV and the XIX centuries, Maori reduced New Zealand's forest cover by about half, largely through controlled fires used to clear land for agriculture.

Nearly 40 species of birds became extinct during this brief period of time. The mass extinction happened because of habitat destruction, hunting and competition with introduced species. Dogs and rats, for example, are species that were introduced to the islands of New Zealand by the Maori. One bird species, the moa, became extinct within a century of human arrival to New Zealand. Moa were giant birds, almost 4 meters tall and 230 kilograms. Giant moa, unable to fly, were such easy prey that the Maori were able to feed large villages with a single bird. Maori began to discard as much as half of the bird's weight as undesirable meat or useless material such as feathers. This wasteful hunting strategy, however, caused the moa to become extinct by about 1400. The extinction of the moa led to the co-extinction of the Haast's eagle, the largest bird of prey ever to have existed. The environment also affected traditional beliefs and cultural practices of the indigenous communities in Australia. Although there are hundreds of indigenous groups native to Australia, these groups use the unified name Aboriginal Australians, or Aborigines.

Aboriginal Australian cultures often had strong spiritual relationships with the local environment. They developed myths to explain the landscape. Modern scientific research has proven that many of these myths are fairly accurate historic records. One series of Aboriginal myths explains that the Australian coastline was once near the edge of the Great Barrier Reef, for example. The reef is now dozens, even hundreds, of meters from the shore. Geologists have proven that this story is accurate. During the last glacial period, when sea levels were lower, Australia's coastline did extend kilometers into what is now the ocean.

Australia and Oceania's vast, ocean-focused geography continues to influence contemporary cultures. Cultural groups and practices focus on uniting peoples and consolidating power in the face of their isolated locations and small populations. These unifying movements are seen at both national and regional levels. Papua New Guinea demonstrates this cultural unification at the national level. The country is one of the most diverse in the world, with more than 700 indigenous groups and 850 indigenous languages. Indigenous groups are explicitly recognized "as viable units of Papua New Guinean society" within the nation's constitution. The constitution also identifies and promotes traditional practices as part of contemporary culture.

The indigenous groups' traditional lands are recognized by the national legislature as customary land title. Customary land title is a recognition that ownership of traditional, tribal land will remain with the indigenous community. Almost all of the land in Papua New Guinea is held with customary land title; less than 3 percent of the land is privately owned.

Indigenous groups regularly work with the government and private companies to harvest the resources on tribal land. Conflicts over land use and resource rights continue to occur between indigenous groups, the government, and corporations.

Cultural practices, especially in sports and the arts, aim to unite Australia and Oceania's isolated peoples at a regional level. Rugby is a very popular sport throughout the continent—more popular than football, baseball, or cricket. Rugby league is the national sport of Papua New Guinea. Rugby union, which has fewer players and slightly different rules than rugby league, is the national sport of New Zealand, Samoa, Fiji, and Tonga.

The tourism industry is the unifying economic force in Australia and Oceania. Tourism is the continent's largest industry, measured by the number of jobs it creates and the money it spreads throughout the Pacific Islands. Tourism, however, also can negatively affect the economies and ecosystems of Australia and Oceania's island nations. It can lead to overcrowding and depletion of isolated islands' scarce resources.

Tourism often focuses on fishing and other recreational water sports. The waters around many Pacific Islands, as well as parts of Australia, have been overfished. Pollution from boats and cruise ships can litter the tropical ocean.

Organizations like the Oceania Sustainable Tourism Alliance aim to promote the sustainable management of natural resources, conserve biodiversity, and adapt to climate change throughout the continent.

CAUCASUS

Caucasus which is considered as historical-ethnographic region has a significant ethnic composition. The ethnic composition of Caucasus nations was formed at the end of bronze and at the beggining of iron ages.

Modern-day there are 3 independent states: Azerbaijan, Georgia (included Abkhazia, Southern Osetia and Adjara provinces), Armenia and also autonomus states attached to Russian Federation: Dagestan, Kabardino-Balkar, Northern Osetia (Alania), Chechenistan, Ingushetian autonomus republics, Adigey autonomus region in Krasnodar, Garachay-Cherkez autonomus province in Stavropol and also Kalmikian autonomus republic which is located on the north-west shores of Caspian Sea. In Caucasus live approximately 50 nations. The largest of them – Azerbaijanis (9 million), Armenians (5 million), Georgians (4 millions), Chechens (1 million), Avars (500 000), Dagestan nations and Lezgins (450 000), Cabardins (350 000), Dargins (320 000) and etc.

Language families. Lingiustically, population of Caucasus belongs to 3 big language families: Caucasus, Indian-Europe and Altay. Minority of these populations who live in Dagestan's territory aren't included to these language families. Russians, Armenians, Ukranians, Tats, Talyshes, Kurds and others represent Indian-Europe language family in Caucasus. Turkic language nations belong to the Altay language family: Azerbaijanis, Nogays, Kumyks, Balkars, Karachays. The most spread language family is Caucasus or Iberian-Caucasus language family. Present-day it is divided into 4 parts:

1. South (Kartvel). Georgians speak in this language.

2. North-west (Abkhaz-Adigey). Abkhazins, Abazins, Adigeys, Cherkezs and Cabardins speak in this language.
3. Central (nakh). Languages of Chechens and ingushes belong to the nakh.
4. Dagestan. Avars, Tabasarans, Dargins, Lezgins and others belong to this part. In Azerbaijan live udins and khynalygs whose languages belong to Dagestan part too.

Antropologically, nations of Caucasus are homogenous, except Nogays and Kalmyks, because they are related to mongoloid type. Others are europoid race. Population is distinguished by 3 features:

1) Colours of hair and eyes
2) Wide face
3) Head index

The clothes of nations of Caucasus have a common character. But there are some differences. Some nations' clothes are similar to eaxh other, for example Abkhazins, Adigeys, Osetins and etc. They wear tight pants, hats, narrow belts and so on.

Religion. According to the religion of Caucasian nations, they are divided into Muslims and Christians. Christianity was spread in the first centuries of AD in Caucasus. In the IV century it was adopted in Armenia, Georgia and Albania. In the VI-VII centuries Christianity was spread among Abkhazins and Adigeys from Georgians. In the VIII century it was accepted by Chechens.

The spread of Islam in Caucasus is related to Arab period (VII-VIII centuries). This religions stengthened here during

Mongol attacks and Timur campaigns. Abkhazins converted to Islam in the XV century during Turkic conquests. In Northern Caucasus Islam was spread mostly by Crimean khans. Because how we know, there were political relations between Ottoman Empire and Crimean khanate. Osetins adopted Islam from Cabarda in the XVII-XVIII centuries. During national-liberation movement of under leadership of Sheikh Shamil Islam was strengthened among nations of North Caucasus.

Georgia. One of the independent states in Caucasus is Georgia. Anthropologically, they are related to the Pont-Zagros type. There were a lot of ethnic groups – Kartli, Kakhet, Imeret, Mokhev, Tushin and etc. But nowadays, they were included to Georgian ethnos and that's why lost their some ethnic features. Mostly, Georgians were engaged in agriculture, cattle-breeding, grape-growing, wine-making, craft. Sledge is one of the national transport vehicles of Georgians. Men's clothes are named chokha-akhalekhi. There is avoided endogamy. When youth wants to marry there must be concluded agreement of dasajerisi. There are 2 kinds of engagement: small-patara and big engagement. The official language of state is Georgian language. The capital of Georgia is a city of Tbilisi. There are also large cities such as Kutaisi and Batumi.

Armenia. The language of Armenians belongs to the Indian-Europe language family. The ancient Armenian language was grabar which was used until the XIX century. From that time, they use new Armenian language-ashkharabar. The capital of Armenia is Erevan.

Armenians came to Caucasus region after Turkmanchay and Adirne treaties. These treaties were signed between Russia and

Iran, Russia and Turkey. According to mentioned treaties Armenians settled in the territories of Irevan and Karabakh which are the ancient Azerbaijani lands. In late 19th Russian Empire created Armenian province in Azerbaijani lands. To this province were included Irevan and Nakhchivan. In 1918 Azerbaijan got independence and could keep its territory Nakhchivan. But Irevan was given to Armenians to create their state. Later in Soviet period some other Azerbaijani territories like Zangazur, Mehri and etc were given to Armenia by Soviet rulers.

Azerbaijan

Azerbaijanis who live in South Caucasus are the largest nation of Caucasus. Traditions, customs, culture have similarities and also diversities from other nations. Modern day the number of population of Azerbaijani Republic is more than 9 million. Except these, Azerbaijanis live in Georgia, Central Asia, Kazakhstan, Russia, Turkey, Iran and etc. as ethnic groups. Generally, in the world live more than 50 million Azerbaijanis. Because of the natural-geographical situation in Azerbaijan, there was creation of great opportunity for development of planting, sericulture, horse-breeding, coppersmith, wood-carving, pottery, carpet-making and etc. Azerbaijan is situated between Europe and Asia and that's why during the centuries culture of Azerbaijan became unique and developed. Azerbaijan is also famous with its national clothes and meals in the world. The official language of Azerbaijan is Azerbaijani language. This language belongs to the Oghuz group of Turkic languages. The territory of republic is about 86 600 square km. Azerbaijan bordering with Russia, Dagestan and Georgia in the north, with Armenia and Turkey in the west, with Iran in the south. 20% of the territory of country was occupied by Armenia. Today, still this conflict (Nagorno-Karabakh) exists. The capital of Azerbaijan is Baku city. Azerbaijan has a rich and long history. On the 28th may of 1918, Azerbaijan gained independence, but after 23 months it was conquered by Bolshevik Russia and forcely was united to the Soviet Union until its collapse on the 18th October of 1991 when Azerbaijan regained its independence. Present-day Azerbaijan is a member of different international organizations and participates in diplomatic missions.

Planting. The natural-geographical situation in Azerbaijan created an opportunity for development of planting culture. Archeological materials prove that here developed gardening and grape-growing. Grain-crops mostly were in the basis of irrigation system. There were 2 forms of planting system:

1. irrigated system (was used in flood-lands)
2. non-irrigated (where extraction of water wasn't possible)

There were also spring-autumn planting systems. Mostly, there was applied to plant wheat. In autumn advantage referred to the yellow, white, red wheat and etc. In Azerbaijan were grown different kinds of paddy. Paddy areas were under water till growing of products. Paddy demands more water than grain-crops. In the 19th century melon plantation developed in Baku, Arash and Goychay gezas. In Lenkeran were grown 23 kinds of melon. Absheron region is famous with its Gala, Zira water-melons. One of the traditional plants of Azerbaijan is cotton. In cotton-planting was applied hired-work. They were people who hadn't lands and came from South Azerbaijan and Dagestan. In Absheron villages are grown saffron. In Guba is still used coloured planting. Gardening and grape-growing emerged in the bronze age. In Azerbaijan are used 4 kinds of growing grapevine.

Sericulture. It has a long history in Azerbaijan. Moses Calancatly mentioned in his "History of Albania" about sericulture in Albania. From the 7th century there were mulberry gardens. In the middle ages, population of Barda, Shirvan and etc. were engaged in sericulture. Arab sources also prove that sericulture developed in Azerbaijan. In XIII-XV centuries, Shaki, Shamakha, Ganja, Tabriz and other regions became the centers of sericulture. During this time, Azerbaijani products were sold in markets of East and West. Great poet Nizami Ganjavi gave information in his works about silk products. We met similar information in works of Khagani. In Shabran mostly was produces raw silk products. European travellers which came to Azerbaijan wrote about the sericulture in Gilan province and merchants of Genua and Venice came here for silk products. Italian traveler - Contarini mentioned that silk of Azerbaijan was sold in markets of Europe and Asia. In the 17th century sericulture developed in Karabakh and there was produced more 10 000 pound silk. Development of sericulture influenced to the economy of Nakhchivan, Maragha, Ardabil and etc. After annexation of North Azerbaijan to Russian empire. Tsarist government made attention to the silk industry. In the 19th century there were produced a lot of silk products in Shusha geza. In this time, from Japan, Bukhara and Khorasan was brought silkwarm to Azerbaijan. Archeological evidences from Mingechevir which related to the II - I millennium BC show that local population used cotton, wool and silk. Azerbaijani products were shown in the exhibitions of Moscow, London and etc. Even were awarded.

Horse-breeding. During the thousands years Azerbaijan people have used horse. Horses played an important role in agriculture of local population and also in military. It's considered as one of the transport vehicles. The history of development of horse-breeding in South Caucasus is related to the Bronze Age. But according the archaeological evidences, we can say that it was also during the Neolithic period. From Mughan, Alikomaktapa were unearthed horse bones. It shows that there were male and female horses 6-7 thousand years age. In research of horse-breeding Gobustan rock carvings also played a main role. There are horse pictures which belong approximately to 4000 years ago. At the end of the 2nd millennium BC and beginning of the first millennium BC horse was considered as a sacred animal. From Nakhchivan, Shakhtakhty village, graves were found all bones of horse. In Nakhchivan, Kultepe monument was found out a figure of horse which has 3000 years. In Mingechevir, from kurgans were unearthed horse bones and also valuable things, belts and etc. According to Assyrian cuneifroms, horse-breeding developed especially during Mannean and Median kingdoms. In Median kingdom, horses of Nisei plain had a great fame. They were quickly and seemed gorgeous. Persian historians wrote in their works interesting facts about these horses. From Ismayilli, Mollaisagli village was found a statue of horse which belongs to the first millennium BC. Geographer-Strabo mentioned about development of horse-breeding during Atropatena and Caucasian Albania.

Art of coppersmith. From the ancient times there existed ore fields in Azerbaijan. There were emeged metallurgy and developed metalworking. Eneolithic evidences show that the first metal was copper. In South Caucasus - Gadabay, Balakan, Dashkesen and etc. were unearthed copper ore fields. The remnants of smelting furnaces were found in Yukhary Dashkesen, Gushchu, Bayan villages. Labor tools of ancient people were very simple. Because they used different kinds of stone. But during the centuries they mixed various minerals and could get other materials. Archeologists found out a lot of bronze in Khodjaly, Shamkir, Urmia and etc. From around of Urmian lake, territory of Mannean kingdom there was unearthed gold bowl (Hasanli) and it proves the development of coppersmith. After the conquest of Azerbaijan by Tsarist Russia, in the 19th century there were many coppersmith shops in Lahij, Baku, Guba, Lenkeran and etc.

Wood carving. The samples of wood carving which were found in Khanlar are related to the end of the 2nd millenium BC. Things made of wood which were unearthed from graves in Mingechevir are related to the beginning of middle ages. Gazvini who lived in the 14th century gave information about wood-carving. In the 17th century French traveler - Sharden wrote about population which engaged in wood carving and made different patterned doors, windows and etc. The centers of wood carving were Guba, Lenkeran, Shamakha, Shaki and etc. In the 17th century merchants of Shamakha sold products made of wood in Astrakhan markets.

Pottery. It's known from the Neolithic period. Experience of pottery had a long history. Emergence of it is related to women. It was developed in eneolithic period, in bronze age was spread and during the centuries, necessity to pottery increased. There appeared also coloured pottery. In the time of feudalism, Barda, Tabriz, Beylagan, Ganja, Nakhchivan and other regions became the centers of pottery. In Guba, Masalli, Lenkeran, Gabala and etc. it's still used.

Jewellery. With the getting of silver and gold jewelry emerged later. There appeared different kinds of jewelry such as brilliant, diamond and etc. Archeological materials were found earings, ring, bracelet, necklace, belt and other decorations. In the middle ages there were silver, gold fields in Azerbaijan. Yagut Hamavi who lived in the 10th century gave information about jewelry in Maragha and Zanjan. In the 17th century European travelers - Sharden, Oleari wrote about gold fields in Sarab. In Azerbaijan different methods was used for making jewelry.

Carpet-making. Azerbaijan people were engaged also in the production of wool, carpet. Emergence of carpet-making is related to the culture of eastern nations. According to the sources of scientists, motherland of carpet-making is Egypt and later it was passed to Asia Minor, Iran, India. Archeological findings show that in the 5-4th centuries BC Median carpets were famous. In the 10th century carpet-making developed in Khoy, Ardabil and Mughan. In the 16th century was established Tabriz miniature school. In the 19th century carpet-making spread in whole South Caucasus. Azerbaijani carpets are distinguished from other carpets with its own decorative style.

BIBLIOGRAPHY

In Azerbaijani

1. Heredot. "Tarix" // tərcümə P. Xəlilov. Bakı. 1998.
2. Həvilov H. A. Azərbaycan Etnoqrafiyası. – Bakı. 1991.
3. Həvilov H. A. Dünya xalqlarının Etnoqrafiyası. – Bakı 1998.
4. Hüseynova S. B. Şərq Slavyanları və Bizans İmperiyası. //
Bakı
Universitetinin Xəbərləri, Humanitar elmlər seriyası №4. 2013.
5. Quliyeva N. Etnoqrafiya və Etnologiya. – Bakı. 2009.
6. Təkləli M. Türk Əsilli Ruslar. Bakı. 2007.

In Russian

7. Бромлей Ю. В. Современные проблемы этнографии: очерки теории и истории. — Москва. 1981.
8. Бромлей Ю. В., Марков Г. Е. Этнография. – Москва. 1982.
9. Бромлей Ю. В. Этнос и этнография. — Москва. 1973.
10. Гуру П. Азия. Москва. 1956.
11. Инал-Ипа Ш.Д. Сухуми. 1960.
12. Очерки общей этнографии. Зарубежная Европа. Москва. 1966.
13. Токарев С.А. История зарубежной Этнографии. – Москва. 1978.
14. Фостер У. Очерк политической истории Америки. Москва. 1965.
15. Харадзе Р.Л. Грузинская семейная община. Тбилиси. 1960.
16. Эленбергер В. Трагический конец бушменов. Пер. с франц. Москва. 1956.
17. Элькин А. Коренное население Австралии. Москва. 1962.

In English

18. Brewer J. D. Ethnography. – Philadelphia. 2000.

19. Kaliszewska I. Everyday life in North Caucasus. Warszawa. 2011.
20. Plokhy S. The Origins of the Slavic Nations. Cambridge University Press. 2006.

Internet sources
21. https://www.ethnologue.com/
22. https://www.britannica.com/
23.https://www.discoveranthropology.org.uk/about-anthropology/fieldwork/ethnography.html
24. http://studopedia.org/8-240370.html